WITHDRAWN FROM STOCK

OVERSHARE

LOVE, LAUGHS, SEXUALITY AND SECRETS

By Rose Ellen Dix
and Rosie Spaughton

Copyright © Redrawr Ltd 2018

The right of Rose Ellen Dix and Rosie Spaughton to be identified as
the authors of this work has been asserted in accordance with the
Copyright, Designs and Patents Act 1988.

This edition first published in Great Britain in 2018 by

Trapeze
an imprint of the Orion Publishing Group Ltd
Carmelite House
50 Victoria Embankment
London EC4Y 0DZ
An Hachette UK Company

1 3 5 7 9 10 8 6 4 2

A CIP catalogue record for this book is available
from the British Library.

ISBN: 978 1 4091 7641 1
Ebook ISBN: 978 1 4091 7642 8

Printed in Great Britain by CPI Group (UK) Ltd, Croydon CR0 4YY

Every effort has been made to fulfil requirements with regard to reproducing
copyright material. The author and publisher will be glad to rectify any omissions
at the earliest opportunity.

www.orionbooks.co.uk

For every LGBT character who deserved better.

CONTENTS

PROLOGUE

ROSIE

Hi, guys! We're Rose and Rosie and we wrote this book you're holding! We're a married couple who share our lives with people on YouTube. Sometimes we like to overshare, but hey, at least you get more than you bargained for – which in reality can be both a blessing and a curse . . .

Over the course of our career online we've had several opportunities to write a book, but we were hesitant. We felt rushed. Most importantly, we felt fraudulent, as neither one of us believed we had enough life experience to begin writing about it. We wanted to make sure we had something to say, as no book is interesting if it doesn't have substance. I mean, what's more disappointing than a chocolate lava cake without the rich, molten mayhem? Who wants a gaping vacuum of emptiness where a book should be, am I right?

We want to take you on a journey, make you laugh at our failings and cry at our stupidity, all the while offering up a slice of our lives that we haven't shared online! Not an easy task when we share so much of ourselves already, but despite the un-reserved nature of our YouTube videos, there is so much we have never revealed – until now. Through our oversharing, we want to remind people that everybody can experience embar-rassment, debilitating self-doubt and rejection in all of its forms, as well as betrayal and heartbreak, and be stronger for it. In this online generation the increasing pressure to appear perfect is overwhelming. How are we expected to evolve without making mistakes? It's unrealistic: everybody has flaws, fractures, inner demons and guilty pleasures, and no one and nothing is perfect – except for us and this book.

ROSE

On our YouTube channels we leave little to the imagination. We're unequivocally candid, honest and outspoken. This has led to our reputation as oversharers. Don't get us wrong, we're far from attention seekers, despite Piers Morgan accusing me of being one because my Twitter bio said 'YouTuber'. Traditional media also seems reluctant to consider that YouTubers might possess intelligence as well as popularity. Imagine that – a new generation of self-sufficient online stars who are not only popular for simply being themselves, but who also project messages of value which could contribute to positive social and political change. But of course, no YouTuber could possibly be in it for the people ... right? Wrong. *We're* in it for the people! Also the money. (Just kidding.)

It's no secret that Rosie and I are visibly out as members of the LGBT community. We were both previously hesitant to write a book that included our own experiences of being bisexual and gay, firstly because these experiences are so personal, and secondly, because we didn't want people to assume we were speaking on behalf of the community as a whole simply because we had a size-able online platform. We've since realised that we needn't have worried. We are speaking on behalf of ourselves, about the issues we've faced together and as individuals, and we have written about them in the hopes of giving strength to those who are facing similar difficulties. We also believe that sometimes just being visibly out can normalise same-sex relationships, without LGBT activism becoming the central focus. What you see online is a true reflection of the relationship we have offline, but needless to say, there is far more to our marriage than the fifteen to twenty minutes we upload each week.

It was never our intention to be quite SO open, it was just the natural trademark of our characters. Give us a camera and we'll give you honesty with a fractional risk of too much information. Give us a livestream and we'll give you hot wind and a monkey bite. Give us a laptop and we'll give you *Overshare*. So why did we write this book? Well, the same reason that Rosie keeps a diary. To be read, to offload, to confide, and to share. We are finally ready to chronicle the best and worst our lives have had to offer, the lessons that we've learned along the way, and the people who have shaped our development – not just to reap the rewards of a book deal and head to Aruba, but to collate stories and experiences that will positively resonate with our YouTube audience *as well as* people who have a life. (You know I'm only joking, guys.)

In this book we've shared things we've never revealed online. The highs and the unbelievable lows, not only in relation to our online rise to 'stardom' (I use quotation marks to emphasise how uncomfortable that word makes me – not because I'm trying to *appear* grounded, but because I genuinely fear sounding like a twat!), but also in relation to growing up, our family lives, our struggles with mental health, and the bittersweet feeling that comes with falling in love.

So here it is, all laid bare for you in the pages ahead! We hope you enjoy this book as much as we've laughed, cried and cringed writing it!

ROSIE

Now, if you're not already a fan: firstly, how dare you?! Secondly, we realise Rose and Rosie are very similar names, so to help you tell us apart we've written this short fact file to get you up to speed. We've also drawn some helpful diagrams to create an extremely detailed image in your mind.

Factfile

ROSE

Dog lover

Perfectionist

Hater of mildew

Obnoxiously well mannered

Can never remember someone's eye colour

Will always remember someone's teeth

Loves Mexican food

Hates cyclists

Always hoovering

Hates to fly but loves to travel

Unintentionally sarcastic

Has a multitude of secret identities connected
by a fictitious story arc

Life motto: 'Stan hard or stay home'

Biggest weakness: the paso doble

Loves: Camila Cabello

Hates: wine snobbery

Worst habit: road rage

Biggest fear: dropping someone else's child
and laughing out of panic

Factfile

ROSIE

Cat lover

Cries at adverts

Addicted to tea

Constantly itchy

Always dropping things

Has read every book ever

Loves everything in miniature

Messy but knows where things are

Obsessed with princess nets

Can pull off any hair colour

Says exactly what she's thinking then instantly regrets it

Life motto: 'What would Pocahontas do?'

Loves: the Spice Girls

Hates: antisocial dog walkers

Worst habit: all of them

Biggest fear: the dark

CHAPTER 1
TEENAGE YEARS

'When you know yourself, it's only yourself
you have to answer to . . . for . . . to . . .'

ROSE

We decided to begin Chapter 1 with our teenage years, since it makes sense to start a story at the beginning rather than at the end. We've all watched films that tease us with scenes out of sequence, leaving us to put together the narrative flow, and who can be bothered with that? Certainly not me, who objects to queueing for ANYTHING, and certainly not Rosie, who's confused about the purpose of the moon. So let's dive straight in! Throughout this book we'll take it in turns to tell our stories. You'll know who's writing from the distinct difference in quality, but for more clarity, it'll say our name just above the section. It's going to be a bumpy ride, so strap yourselves in, put on your 3D glasses, and enjoy the road ahead! (Just so everyone's clear, there's no need for the glasses. They're just an optional extra.)

My teenage years were by far the most pivotal and painful years of my life. But once I'd got to grips with the responsibilities that came with my spider bite, even tougher times raised their ugly heads. School was a mixed bag of emotions. Like a packet of misshapen liquorice allsorts with body-confidence issues. I say liquorice allsorts because they're the most undesirable of confectionary, and this bag of emotions possessed particularly undesirable contents. I have an extremely anxious disposition, and being so highly strung as an adult is how I was awarded the nickname 'High Alert'. For as long as I can remember, sudden cold-sweated panic has been an intrinsic part of my life. But, perhaps ironically, the process of realising and accepting I was gay caused me little concern. It felt so familiar and normal to me growing up that I valued it as one of the best parts of myself. I had so much love to give and I couldn't understand how that could ever be perceived as disgusting or amoral.

Being a teenager was an uncertain and greasy stage of my development. These are the crucial years of self-discovery, and I discovered two very important things about myself. One, I was strongly attracted to women. And two, wearing your sister's hand-me-down leather jacket on non-uniform day doesn't automatically make you better than Miss Dork, the music teacher with aggressively protruding front teeth (who deserves respect despite her cartoon aesthetic). As a thirteen-year-old I thought there wasn't anything more amusing than Miss Dork's dorky appearance – until I was struck by the hilarity of my own name. I was Miss Dix with no interest in men. LOL.

Growing up, I could switch from extremely confident to painfully self-conscious in seconds. School was uncomfortable. I didn't help myself by starting Year 7 with the most unforgivable haircut in the history of evolution: the hybrid of moose and Deirdre Barlow was perplexing and antagonistic for people. The world wasn't ready for gender boundaries to be pushed quite that far, and it didn't set me up well for seamless social integration. My design technology teacher mistook me for a boy, which led to a cacophony of giggles that were so in sync they harmonised into a choral shattering of my soul. It was worse than the time I publicly dumped Tom Bennett and then some brute threw a sandwich at him just to make sure he was really down. He cried. Cheese can be weighty. Especially in middle-class sandwiches, when a mature cheddar can be as thick as half an inch. The school playing fields can be tough, so yummy mummies often pack their children's lunch boxes with food that can also double up as a weapon. Never underestimate the tripping power of a chilled linguine or the ricochet of a dried apricot. I've learned many lessons of how to survive in a nineties and noughties secondary school, some of which are still applicable today. Let me elaborate . . .

Tips to Survive High School

■ Never admit to having sandwiches made from a 50/50 loaf. It's weak and weakness leads to isolation. Isolation leads to Boyz II Men and Boyz II Men leads to nowhere good.

■ If you're going to be a part of the scooter or diabolo crazes, you need to choose where your loyalties lie. In the early 2000s you couldn't have more than one interest at a time – that would make you far too complex to understand, and multifaceted people weren't to be trusted.

■ If you want to go home and need to fake an illness, always go with 'I'm hearing voices.' Zero visible symptoms and a 100 per cent success rate.

■ If you're going to trade lunch box goods, know your margins. Never trade for 'baked' crisps or peaches. That's an unfulfilling excuse for a carb, and fruit with fur is suspicious. Choose household names and nothing too exotic. If someone offers you diced pineapple cubes presented in a freezer bag, tell them to get the fuck out your face.

■ Modify your uniform enough to be cool, but be clever enough not to break the rules. If you untuck your shirt all the way, you've lost this challenge and now you're the sewer rats of Livingstone house, the lowest and most challenged of creatures.

■ Perfect the art of the 'messy bun' (a concept I could never execute – my personality traits hugely conflicted with the skills needed to accomplish this look).

■ Social circles: be friendly to all but commit to none. Never be someone's number two. Rosie hates it.

■ Avoid extra-curricular chess.

■ If you have excess saliva try to contain it. Never have I forgotten the names of people I've met with this issue.

■ If you're in love with your best friend you're fucked: don't do it.

As I entered secondary school I was placed in Cheshire house, which was notoriously shit but no shitter than Shaftesbury. Shaftesbury was Hufflepuff, Cheshire was Ravenclaw. My brother and sister were both in Ashley house, known for its bloodthirsty inter-house athletics, esteemed social circles, and Jenny Cooke, daughter of French teacher Mrs Cooke (who struck a striking resemblance to Katrina and the Waves). The reason I chose to be placed in Ravenclaw followed a story that involves my high-school taster day, carrot sticks and public vomiting. I simply couldn't have recovered and needed a fresh start.

My sister's immaculate reputation amongst the teachers at Bishops made life very easy for me when I joined the school. Laura was an exemplary student. Her ambitions and ability to apply herself later landed her at Cambridge University – the biggest success story of our family until I absolutely smashed her accomplishments with my fame. John was more of a slow burner but was able, with a little guidance from my mother. 'Guidance' being the generous way of describing it . . . Mum spoon-fed John so vigorously throughout his GCSEs that I think he swallowed the spoon. One of my memories growing up as a young teenager involves disgruntled murmurs from the dining room, where Mum had backed him into a corner, both figuratively and literally, during a particularly hostile interrogation on electromagnetic force. In fact, most of my early memories revolve around John's GCSE revision – but let me continue with Laura. Her angelic clean slate gave me the ultimate head start, and I was soon known as Laura Dix's little sister, heir to the Snoot throne. It was my ticket in, so to speak – I needn't have bothered trying to prove myself to members of staff as Laura's reputation was my free pass to Special Treatment Town.

Laura and I were inseparable growing up. If she'd had enough playing Lego Paradisa, I'd had enough. If she wanted to come in from outside, I wanted to come in from outside. If she questioned why John's Lego men had American accents, I questioned why John's Lego men had American accents. Poor John, he needed a brother . . . and a gentle reminder of the country we were born in.

From a young age Laura was always concerned for our welfare. I was too young to recall her reaction when we lost John on the beach at St Ives, but I can imagine her meltdown when he was found. Laura liked to look after us both, and growing up she became my telephone voice inspiration. Never have I met someone with the ability to construct and deliver such perfectly executed sentences in the most regal intonation.

Her delivery shook me to my very core. I have learned many a lesson from Laura's example. The first: work hard because it always pays off. And the second: don't flirt with Spiros the Spanish holiday rep if you're not prepared for his unanticipated arrival in England. I had a lot of time for Laura – but not while she was bedridden for weeks with glandular fever. Her cries of discomfort bothered me some. But I found that by closing her door her wails were silenced and the problem went away. That was merely payback for the time she adopted the personality of an abandoned cat called Maw-Maw and duped me into giving her the last of my Opal Fruits. Little did I know, Maw-Maw wasn't to be sympathised with, never have I met such a calculating, emotionally manipulative feline.

Laura played a huge part in my development as a teenager. Mum never had to push her to revise or bribe her with pick 'n' mix. After a particularly grafting weekend writing an essay on the Abyssinia Crisis, our first family computer crashed and Laura lost forty-eight hours of work. I'd never seen someone take their frustrations with technology out on their own head. She had nothing else to hit, and this time her screams couldn't be silenced by closing the door. We left her to grieve but made sure frozen peas were available for the trauma. I was in awe of her commitment to academia. Like me, Laura is a perfectionist, an over-analyser, and a spiritualist. John, however, was an over-eater, a *Power Rangers* enthusiast, and was blissfully unaware of the impact of his constantly being the centre of negative attention. Am I resentful? Absolutely. Do I fashion it into comedy to mask the pain? Sure do! This is partly why I took such delight in winding him up, which could often lead to quite violent ends. The art of running to the bathroom and locking the door to avoid being swept into his tornado of teenage aggression was something I mastered. When he and Mum argued, it was best to migrate or leave the hemisphere. John's I WANT mentality was what frustrated me the most, but the sulks that formed in the aftermath of a rejected request were the comedic silver lining to a draining situation.

I do feel sorry for John. Perhaps Laura and I inadvertently excluded him growing up. I remember on one of our annual Caravan Club holidays, I decided to use my bicycle to create my own taxi service. I called it 'Rose's Roads'. I'd let Laura jump on the back of my bike and around the campsite we'd go! I was inspired by 'Laura Lines', where I'd jump into the inflatable dinghy at Babbacombe Beach and Laura would paddle me down the shore. John wanted his own travel service, so he decided to patent 'John's Jumbo Jets'. Unfortunately, he soon realised he couldn't provide anyone with what the service claimed to offer as he had none of the resources available. It was a short-lived luxury service, and one that needed slightly more funding.

Everyone remembers their first celebrity crush. Mine was Leonardo DiCaprio in *Titanic*. I kissed the poster I had on my wall so many times the paper went crusty. My second was Jennifer Aniston as Rachel from *Friends*. It seemed I was attracted to everyone – boys, girls, it didn't matter. It was something I didn't even question, let alone worry about. Throughout primary and secondary school I developed crushes on both girls and boys, but I do remember how different my feelings felt towards each sex. I'm going to do my best to describe it. When it came to boys, I liked the way I felt safe and protected – which is absolutely ridiculous and goes against everything I believe in as an adult! It didn't really go beyond that. Boy attraction was more of a single-layered fondness rather than an exhilarating, all-absorbing existential crisis of a girl-on-girl love affair. For me, attraction to men was blancmange: the thought of it was neither pleasing nor displeasing – it was perfectly average – but it was no mango-and-cardamom syllabub. It lacked layers, the sweet, the sour, the mint garnish and the posh porcelain. Girls had attitude, they had flavour. They had a depth that I couldn't reach with men. I'm not saying men aren't deep, I'm saying I couldn't be bothered to abseil.

But love is a serious topic. Some say it makes the world go round. (Scientists might argue that it has no bearing on the earth's twenty-four-hour spin cycle, but my cynicism of scientific fact has skyrocketed since I read that they have created a functioning guitar the size of a human blood cell. A necessary use of time and resources, sure, but I'll only believe it when they've found someone small enough to win Best Breakthrough Artist.) It's my opinion that love certainly makes the ride worthwhile, and if I were to write a harrowing Tumblr-style definition of it, it would read as follows:

> 'Love is like type 2 diabetes:
> you could lose a part of yourself.'
> **ROSE ELLEN DIX**

Mildly offensive, yes, but truer words have never been spoken. Arguable, but even so, you'll find that love has many similarities to diabetes. Frequent urination, slow to heal, and, like type 2, love can blind you. I'm a strong believer that love is love regardless of your gender or sexuality. In the words of the late Meg Ryan, 'Love is the bridge between all our differences.' I'm aware Meg Ryan is yet to pass but the evolution of her face leads me to believe she's at least tardy and I have no evidence of her saying this quote. But despite that succession of disjointed thoughts, the message remains the same: love cannot be hateful, it doesn't discriminate, it looks beyond mere externals, and it's the one commonality that binds our differences. Let's transcend into my own fantastically tragic experiences, shall we? Now, I'm gay. I'm also Gemini, a Slytherin, a Monica Lewinsky stunt double, a parkour specialist, a former mall Santa, and a mistruster of horses. In my opinion, my preference for women has no bearing on how my experience of love can be related to, regardless of it being a steamy same-sex shenanigan. However, there are naturally aspects of it that will resonate most strongly with the LGBT community.

I first fell in love at eighteen years old. It turns out my feelings for Pugwall as a child were mere infatuation and fashion resentment.

When I was four the love I felt for Tim, a fleeting holiday fixation, was also temporary. I was tantalised by his nineties centre parting and refusal to ride a bike with mudguards, that sexy courageous bastard. At five the love I felt for Ben was shaken by a passionate disagreement about our future. It was break time, and Mrs Calderbank was busy preparing for an afternoon of painting paper plates for no educational purpose. Meanwhile Ben thought recess was the perfect opportunity to tell me he was leaving me for a life in the forces. I didn't want him to risk his life for our queen and country, and I made that quite clear. I've always been a girl who speaks her mind, but my objection to his career ambition led to a cruel white paint/PVA glue stunt, which ruined my paintbrush and eradicated my ability to trust. He knew exactly how to hurt me ... Fortunately the next day we were over it and were back in our kissing box, a cardboard box with no windows and no interruptions. But a graphic game of Doctor led to an uncomfortable conversation with our parents and I haven't heard from him in sixteen years. Then there was William. He cut me deeply. Don't be mistaken, this wasn't the result of an emotional estrangement, merely an almighty gash through my thumb during a merciless game of scissor swords. The blood that gushed from my hand was enough to make Mrs Calderbank drop her stick insects in hysteria. She reacted practically by shouting in delirium until the blood was too frightened to continue to flow. William and I had our differences. Our relationship could never have blossomed into anything romantic after the night I told him to get out of my life when a play fight ended violently. William lost his hair and I lost my self-respect.

Stephen was wonderful. Charming, theatrical, hilariously quick-witted, and flamboyantly gay. I didn't realise that at the time, just like I hadn't realised it about myself, and perhaps that's why Stephen was my longest primary-school relationship. We were committed to each other for two years. We made it official when we got married by the poplar tree, and then renewed our vows a year later after a rocky patch involving a third party (I'm not ready to talk about Isaac or his reptiles). Stephen taught me what it really meant to care about another person, by allowing me to drive his electric child-sized car. Around the middle-class estate we zoomed at a reckless 5mph, with the wind in our hair and not a care in the world. His passion for *Westside Story* and a perfumed collar were some of the things I admired most about him. But none of these early relationships were love.

I had several crushes throughout secondary school but they were more difficult to disguise because they were predominantly focused on women. Boys didn't interest me much – apart from Ben, who had grown into a stunning young entrepreneur. During Year 7 form room he would sell sweets he'd bought at the local shop to other students. But his inflated margins were totally unreasonable and far beyond the recommended retail price. His dubious and somewhat fraudulent trade practices discouraged me from our primary-school dreams of marriage. I couldn't rely on such a loose cannon with criminal leanings, and even at eleven years old I understood that no woman should have to be provided for with immorally acquired money. No woman should have to be provided for full stop, but I was too young to grasp feminism (or at least pretend to understand it like I do now to stay relevant and appear cultured and hip).

In the first year of secondary school it was uncool for boys to acknowledge girls, but we soon had the upper hand when diablos were banned at lunch break. Suddenly we became extremely valuable commodities. For a boy, having a girlfriend or two showed dominance, removing the need to urinate on prize cafeteria or playground territory. But while other girls aspired to it, I didn't want to be someone's trophy wife, and I was secretly upset that diablos had become contraband. Like the boys, I thought balancing an object on a string was a breakthrough in recreational entertainment, and I much preferred that than being the object of their affections. But before long, girls became far more interesting to me too. I don't know if it was the air of mystery or the cheap Impulse I could smell, but I liked it.

Love was never something I allocated much thought to until I saw how difficult it was for Buffy Summers. She was in love with a vampire, which was inconvenient at best, but she stayed true to herself in the face of adversity, and killed him when he became bothersome and a threat to world order. Fortunately, death was only a semi-permanent hurdle, and once Angel was back from Hell they continued to make it work. I learned many things from that television show; that murder wasn't the only way to resolve an issue, and that interspecies relationships were often frowned upon. All of which were valuable lessons, but Buffy's attraction to the forever-young homicidal undead proves that love occurs in the unlikeliest of places, and a sword through the heart and 100 years of hellfire doesn't necessarily thwart it. Love is not something you can control, and without conscious thought you can become its house elf, aka ugly little bitch. For me, the feelings I had for girls were far more intense than any I had experienced before. More intense than my hatred for any Matt Damon franchise or for people who pronounce assumed 'ashoomed'.

Boys were like a flavourless casserole, while girls were the red wine *jus* to the commonplace gravy granule, the Lumière to a non-French-speaking candle and the Fritz Bernaise to a low-end fictional fashion designer. They had a quality that was so intriguing to me that at first I thought it was jealousy I was feeling, or simply the compounds of friendship, but when I bought the same washing powder as one of my female fancies so that I could bask in her fragrance (which reminded me of meadows, a harpsichord and the emotional comfort of springtime) – I realised that was a little gay. A lot gay. Billie Jean King grand-slamming gay.

With women everything was both more exciting and more gentle. I didn't feel intimidated by boys, I felt bored by them. Believe it or not, growing up I had few internal struggles with being gay. It didn't really make much difference to me, and naively, I never thought it would affect any of my job ambitions, because why would it? If you're an actress, being straight doesn't mean you can't play gay, so why on earth would it be any different the other way around?

Having said I didn't have much internal struggle, at fifteen years old – as I was beginning to develop my painfully analytical mind – my conscience kicked in, and I started feeling horribly guilty for having romantic feelings for my friends. I started to think that I was behaving badly by keeping it a secret, that I was luring them into a false sense of security, and that my silence only proved that I had reason to feel ashamed. If they found out, I feared they would treat me differently (which I can guarantee would have been the case). My confidence was shaken. Not because I was unsure of myself, but quite the opposite. I was sure I was heading down the rainbow road to Homosexual City, population unknown, and either I had to accept that or fight it. This period of questioning my moral code lasted for four months. During that time I wanted to feel better about myself in a way I could control, and I developed an eating disorder which had a dramatic effect on my body. Every day I would survive on one bacon sandwich for breakfast and a small evening meal. I had nothing to eat at school, which soon caused alarm to Head of House, Mrs Moody (who was ironically the kindest lady you'll ever meet).

I weighed 7 stone, had no energy, no colour in my skin, and no time for people telling me I looked unwell. Were they mad?! I LOOKED GREAT. My ribs made music like steel drums and I was invisible when I turned sideways. The only downside was the beard I grew as my body hair tried to protect my dwindling extremities, but beard or no beard, I felt oddly confident every time someone pointed out how much weight I'd lost. During this fragile time I tried to convince myself that my attraction to men was stronger than anything I felt for women. I even made a pros list in their favour . . . it wasn't extensive:

Men: Pros

Can't spell 'women' without 'men'

Fortunately, I soon returned to a healthy weight once I was more confident in my own skin. (It was also a result of my mother bribing me to revise for my GCSEs. I couldn't help but be seduced by tempting E numbers and conspiring carbohydrates to get me through the workload, and I needed the glucose to secure my grades.) After a year of struggling as a stick insect, I somehow managed to prevent my behaviour from spiralling into anything more serious. But little did I know how my compulsive disposition and obsessional need for control would later manifest as something else . . .

My crush on Nicole Kidman as Satine in *Moulin Rouge* was causing me great concern. Firstly, because she had tuberculosis. Secondly, because she was a woman. I was obsessed with this film and wanted to believe it was down to my passion for musical theatre, but then I realised that that was probably pretty gay in itself, so I decided to give in, stop fighting the fight, and 'Come What May'. One thing I will say against the film is that Nicole lied when she sang 'Diamonds Are a Girl's Best Friend': in hindsight, a better friend would have been a cure for the illness that killed her. Nonetheless, I learned many valuable lessons from this musical extravaganza. I learned that love shouldn't ever be quelled. That love is powerful and good, no matter who it's between. That everyone deserves it, and that it cannot possibly be measured or deemed anything other than equal. I took that last revelation and ran with it. Well, I didn't *run* with it because of my low blood sugar and borderline anorexia, but figuratively, I ran with it.

I vividly remember the day I walked into school feeling comfortable in my own skin and at peace with being different – although a little anxious that other people would be able to tell or would notice a change in me. No one did, probably because they were too focused on sensible Pokémon trades and canteen politics. It felt so freeing to allow myself to be happy. For me, coming out felt entirely unnecessary at that point in my life. I saw no immediate benefit of the emotional strain that would surely ensue. I also wasn't ready to share this secret with anyone other than myself, and I began to think of it more as a privilege to be earned rather than a confession I had to spit out. My decision not to go public wasn't because I felt ashamed; it was because I wanted to enjoy being the only one who knew. A big part of self-discovery is getting to know the real you. So I wanted to take the time to get to know myself before I went and put a label on it.

Having said that, it was becoming more difficult to hide, especially from the ones who loved me the most. I knew Laura knew. And I think she knew I knew she knew. But it wasn't until I was sixteen that I thought the time was right to tell her. Looking back, I wish I'd done it more dramatically, in the form of puppeteering, or a Broadway number, or with the help of a flash mob, but those weren't viable options, and the circumstances were slightly more complex than simply wishing to get it off my chest. Sixteen was also the age I realised I suffered from obsessive compulsive disorder, later to be confirmed by a series of professionals. Telling Laura I was gay seemed far easier than trying to explain my intrusive thoughts and the way my brain was tragically malfunctioning. I felt I had to tell Laura, so she could help me figure out whether being gay was in any way linked to the hell I was going through. Two analytical minds were surely better than one! Her reaction was what I had always predicted. She knew and was totally supportive of it. Just as supportive as she'd been of my decision to throw her first ever boyfriend a paper aeroplane with a black spot drawn on it. We both knew he wasn't the one, and he needed a pirate's warning so he'd get the message.

Coming out to my mother wasn't quite as easy. Being gay in theory was much more acceptable to her than being gay in practice. To the delight of my father, a lot of my mum's former colleagues at the BBC were gay, and she'd often say, 'I don't *hate* gays, Rose — [*blank*] was gay.' Well, unfortunately [blank] wasn't around to back my corner. My mum wasn't alone in her discomfort with having a gay daughter. I remember a close friend once telling me that it was fine for me to stay over at her house: her mum didn't mind that I was gay, just as long as *she* wasn't. Believe it or not, that was said to comfort me! I think a lot of people want to appear as though they're exceptionally open-minded and liberal, but as soon as there's a hint of a feather boa in their immediate family, their attitudes change.

Mum didn't find it easy. It wasn't so much a discomfort with my attraction to women as it was concern about the way I might be treated by others. You have to consider that parents have a preconceived idea of how your life will turn out, and anything that meanders from that is unknown, and that can be scary. I don't resent her for it – everyone is entitled to react honestly. Remember that you've had your entire life to get to a place of comfort and pride, and to expect that in a second from your parents could be asking too much. A hesitant or even negative reaction doesn't mean they don't love you unconditionally; just allow them the time you gave yourself during all those years of hardship and struggles. So my advice to anyone who doesn't receive the positive reaction they wanted is to give it time. I never thought my mum would ever be comfortable enough to plan my wedding, invite Rosie and me on holidays abroad, or discuss baby daddy sperm donors! Never underestimate someone's ability to alter their views when it comes to love.

My first experience of love left me with a bitter taste in my mouth. But I soon realised it wasn't love itself that caused me pain (that part made every day as exciting as a Camila Cabello album release), it was the fact that I was led on – or, rather, that I entirely misjudged the situation, to my own spectacular failing.

I'm sure many of you will relate to seeing signs of requited love when actually they don't exist at all. Love makes you crazy like that. You over-analyse every interaction and rose-tint it into an extract from a power-ballad music video. You spend every second ruminating over what you said, how they reacted, momentary physical contact, lingering stares, and their mysterious emotional damage that you find so hot. Just me? God, I love a broken woman. I think it's a lesbian thing – because we love our drama – but there's nothing I find more attractive than a tortured babe with emotional baggage. Throw in some Cuban/Mexican heritage and you're golden. Oh, you need fixing? ME, I CAN DO THAT. I'M THE ONLY ONE FOR THE JOB. NO ONE UNDERSTANDS YOU LIKE I DO. Why do I find girls in tragic disrepair so attractive? It's actually a bit messed up. All I want to do is be the person who sorts out their shit and straightens out their life, just as long as it isn't really arduous and time-consuming.

ROSIE

I can re-break myself, just so you know . . .

ROSE

Let's talk about Bliv. I'm calling her Bliv because her real name is Liv and that small amendment means she can remain anonymous.

I met Bliv when I was eighteen when we were studying at art college together. Bliv's knack for making every day a jovial and vivacious affair was exactly what I needed. She was fashionable, hilarious and independent. I was only one of those things. We really hit it off and became very close very fast. I pulled a classic move and told Bliv I was bisexual, to appear less predatory. I like to think of it as 50 per cent true, so before you judge me for contributing to bi-erasure, perhaps I should actually be admired for my perfectly even ratio of truth to lie. A lot of gay people use the same 'partial admission' as a way of alleviating the shock of coming out. This 'stepping stone' technique angers real bisexuals because it appears to invalidate their true identity, and although this might seem amusing to some, it's not to me. You'll never catch me trolling my wife or her transient sexual proclivity.

I'm not saying Bliv would have been perturbed by my gayness, but I didn't want her to assume that our friendship meant more to me than it did to her. I thought identifying as bisexual would make me seem provocative, dangerous and *en vogue* – like Katniss Everdeen but without the brutal killing and heterosexual love interest.

Either way, Bliv was unfazed, and so began months of painful analytical reasoning in favour of reciprocated feelings where there was certainly only evidence of probable cause. In this case the crime committed was disturbing the peace – of my HEART. Also indecent exposure, because I saw more than I should have.

Like me, I'm sure many of you have misjudged a situation from time to time. Like assuming the Gilmore Girls were dating and not related, or thinking that *Pretty Little Liars* would get better with time. During a maths test I once read each question as the multiplication of a decimal number, not realising that the question number came before a full stop, neither of which were part of the actual question.

1. $4 \times 3 =$
'OMG, HOW DO I CALCULATE THIS?'

2. $7 \times 8 =$
'WHAT IS TWO POINT SEVEN TIMES EIGHT? OH GOD!'

3. $9 \times 6 =$
'I ONLY REVISED BASIC MULTIPLICATION! WTF, I'M NOT MATT DAMON!'

Sometimes it's easy to see things that aren't really there. I think for many of us there's a morbid fascination in falling for people we know aren't right for us or who aren't even remotely attainable. I'm an absolute sucker for wanting something I can't have, which is why my relationship with dairy is such a torment (dairy, you irresistible bitch). The more I starve my dog of attention the more she wants to French kiss my mouth. The more someone ignores me the more I want to appear unclothed in their pantry. It's a bizarre cognitive conundrum which causes us the kind of pain we want more of, a similar pain to a wobbly tooth; it's moreish and bittersweet. Like a lemon cheesecake with an ambiguous best-before date, and with potentially catastrophic consequences. We want to get hurt because feeling pain, whether it's physical or emotional, confirms that we're living, so perhaps as a species we are seeking certification of our existence. How can we appreciate the highs without suffering the lows?

I was watching a wildlife programme last night, because I like to renarrate natural-history documentaries with relevant social commentary. As I was voicing 'Brian' the disorderly flamingo with a history of violence, I asked Rosie why things have to die in order for other creatures to live. Rosie responded with, 'Don't know. Refill my bottle for me, I need to drink more water in general.' That got me thinking. The world is a cruel place. Nature, the food chain and survival of the fittest are actually incredibly brutal. I said to Rosie, 'Here's your water, but do you think without suffering we would still be able to recognise happiness?' And she said, 'No. Are you going to finish that ice cream?'

That also got me thinking: are we capable of falling completely and defencelessly in love without ever having had our hearts thoroughly stamped on? Or, on the flip side, does having our hearts broken impede our ability to emphatically love someone, because we're always on the defensive? More importantly, are these questions anyone cares about or should I just tell an unrelated joke at Italy's expense? The latter? Cool. What's a specimen? An Italian astronaut. There's just never an opportunity to tell that joke because specimen isn't a common topic of conversation and I have no Italian friends. Although this is probably why.

I was in love with Bliv for about a year without her knowing, and I was fairly positive she had similar feelings to me. Not love, but perhaps a diluted fondness, like weak Ribena. I could tell by the way we'd snuggle and talk about our feelings. When she broke up with her indie beansprout boyfriend I was certain something would happen. Of course I never had the confidence to tell her the truth about how I felt: I've never been confident or assertive when it comes to women. I'd never want to appear predacious or assuming. I don't even know how to flirt. If I'd not made the biggest blunder in text message history, she'd never have known the truth. She reacted exceptionally well when I sent her the wrong message, which stated how hard it was seeing her flirt with Toby Pony (a boy named Toby who strongly resembled a pony). The cat was out of the bag.

So, to summarise: teen years were difficult, emotionally gruelling, and nothing ever happened with Bliv. I deleted her off Facebook and regretted it. But as the saying goes, 'We always hurt the ones we love.' Just look at Patrick Swayze in *Ghost*. He had no regard for Demi's pot. He purposefully ruined it from the safety of the afterlife in a quest to quash the only hobby she'd had since his tragic passing. Cruel. And look at Kate Winslet. There was plenty of room on that piece of wood and everyone knows it. She could have taken a coffee flask and some crustless cucumber sandwiches and there still would have been room. Not only do I feel for Jack in this situation, but also for the husband Rose went on to marry, who didn't appear in her idyllic portrayal of the afterlife. I can only assume he was in steerage and not allowed to celebrate the quelling of his mortal coils by the clock.

I hadn't intended this chapter to be all about my experiences, until I realised how interesting I am. That would be true if 'interesting' and 'nothing special' meant the same thing. Regardless of that debate, only the most esteemed authors reflect on their experiences to substantiate and expand their discussion. Is that true? It sounds plausible, but what do I know? I'm a YouTuber, not an academic, despite my first-class honours degree, extensive vocabulary, Secret Service potential and unmistakable modesty. What I like most about writing a book is that you can present anything as fact, because someone's trusted you enough as a writer to bind your words together and make them available to purchase, which automatically inflates their prestige and validates their content. For example, if I were to tell you that Chloë Grace Moretz stole my sitar, or that Chelsea Handler told me I pronounced 'taco' weirdly, you'd believe it – and you should because one of those is true.

My teenage years were certainly the most difficult ones I've had to endure, but strangely they're ones I look back on with fondness. There's nothing like cracking a smile at your own bumpy evolution while toasting your accomplishments with friends like Hindsight (a nice guy, but only tends to show up *after* you need him).

ROSIE

I'm writing this chapter while on a flight to Los Angeles, because there's nothing like lack of sleep, brooding music and hours and hours to contemplate your life choices to get you in the mood. Am I paranoid that the people sitting behind me are reading this over my shoulder? Yes I am.

I knew that I was bisexual when I was ten. I can remember having a mad crush on not one but TWO girls in primary school, who happened to be best friends. Then when I went to high school I met a girl outside the mobile history block who told me she was a lesbian and we struck up a friendship. I was lucky to meet somebody who was so young and yet so sure of her sexuality, and so vocal about it. Growing up with a very liberal mum, I didn't actually realise what homophobia was, and the extent to which it could affect people. Although I do remember noting that nobody else claimed to be gay – I didn't know any gay adults – and, at the time, the word 'gay' itself was used as an insult by everybody, including me.

Because I didn't have any awareness of how being bisexual, or gay, or LGBT could affect my life, I was fairly confident with it, and would often say how fit women were, or when a girl at school looked good I would be first to comment. I didn't ever hide because I didn't feel like I had to – or even realise that there might be a reason to do so.

I can remember telling a fellow waitress I worked with that I was bi and her telling me that she already knew, and that was the reaction I got from everyone. The worst reactions I ever had were people being dismissive, which is what my mum was guilty of when I tentatively told her that I thought I could be bisexual at about fourteen. I never worried that she would react badly, but I felt awkward bringing it up because it's just generally awkward discussing sexual things with a parent! She brushed it off, perhaps because she felt equally awkward, and said something about me being 'too young to know what I was yet'. I can remember thinking, 'Actually, I'm very confident that I know what I am,' and we didn't discuss it again until much later.

When another girl in my class came out as bi I remember feeling like I had an ally, but then hearing other people scoff that she was 'only doing it for attention' made me wonder if that was what my classmates thought about me too.

When I was fifteen I went to an under-sixteens night at a club called the Void. My friends and I had a competition about who could kiss the most people, and I won with a landslide record of thirteen: twelve boys and one girl called Dani, who I became OBSESSED with. It turned out Dani was super rich and had a massive house with horses, and I considered her to be a princess and would sit and stare at her MySpace all day.

But then I started spending more and more time hanging out with the girl I had met outside the history block, and would often go to her house and watch *Desperate Housewives*. I felt we were getting closer. I wanted to go out with her, but I was nervous. Even though I felt confident in my own sexuality, I had never really put it into practice. I didn't know what to do with a girl, and there was nowhere I could really learn (although I had watched *Tipping the Velvet*, so I was at somewhat of an advantage despite my lack of Victorian apparatus). She asked me out, and I said yes! I felt really happy about it. But walking home from school that day, I told a friend who was extremely religious. She told me that I shouldn't do it, that it wasn't right and would go horribly wrong. She told me to end it. I walked away feeling dirty and embarrassed, and the next day I met up with my new girlfriend before school. She said, 'You're going to end it, aren't you?' I just nodded. Looking back, I wish I'd been stronger, but with my own nervousness muddled with the guilt and shame my friend had made me feel, I just couldn't do it. However, despite not having an 'official' relationship, we spent our school years flirting outrageously and low-key experimenting with one another. It was officially unofficial.

In school I had a reputation. Malvern is a small town where everyone knows everyone. But people in the years below me knew my name even when I didn't know theirs. (Apart from Richard Richardson, who just happened to be the son of Richard Richardson. So Richard Richardson's SON. Everybody knew his name.) I was definitely talked about. I was extremely self-assured, headstrong and didn't give a shit about what other people thought. I literally didn't even contemplate other people's opinions of me, it never even crossed my mind to do so. I was far too busy chasing boys to worry about that. I can remember my German teacher announcing in front of the class that he had caught me kissing not one, not two, but THREE different boys in the space of a school week. I was so proud, despite not receiving any form of certificate.

Maybe it was growing up with two older brothers, but I felt totally in control and unfazed when it came to boys. In fact, I felt that I could wrap them around my little finger. This sexual confidence didn't go unnoticed by my peers, and unfortunately I was often slut-shamed. What's crazy is that I was actually put into the category of 'slut' before I'd even lost my virginity. Throughout my entire school life I only slept with one guy: my boyfriend Barney, who I had a relationship with on and off for about four years. Not that I need to justify myself in any way. Whether I'd been sexually intimate with zero guys or a thousand, people had no right to try and shame me to lower my self-confidence. Ironically, on the final day of school, almost every guy who'd ever teased me tried to hook up with me in a shameless last-ditch attempt. Sorry, boys, you don't deserve me.

I was happy in myself at school, despite the fact that my home life was far from perfect. I felt that I looked good, but back then there certainly wasn't the same pressure on young people to look perfect as there is today. There was no Instagram, or Snapchat. No Kardashians. I never weighed myself or even considered my own weight and what that could mean. I'm not saying that there wasn't ANY pressure, I'm just saying that it was definitely a different time. I would just walk into school and rock it. I rolled my skirt up as high as I physically could. In sixth form I would often wear a see-through skirt to school. During the winter it was fine because I wore black tights underneath, but then one summer's day I wore it with no tights and got sent home – but I still wore it again the next day. Perhaps it was all those years of listening to the Spice Girls talk about girl power, but I just didn't give a shit.

I skipped the queue in the canteen, I always fought back even if I was wrong, and if someone pissed me off I would cut them out. Burning bridges was actually my speciality: I didn't even pause to see if I missed someone, I just kept going. I had a line and few people dared cross it.

My mum and dad had my two elder brothers, Tom and William, then me, and divorced when I was three. My dad would come and visit us at weekends, but that started to happen less and less. He lived and worked in Milton Keynes and we lived in Malvern. To a child, that's very, very far away. He ended up remarrying a woman who already had three children, and they all took his last name. He stopped sending us birthday cards, Christmas cards, and he left a massive Dad-shaped hole in my heart. One Christmas I rang him and his wife answered and told me he couldn't come to the phone because he was playing with his new family.

I was broken and conflicted and too young to really understand that sometimes things just don't work out. I grew up an absolute romantic, always on the lookout for real, true love but fearful of commitment. My dad's leaving turned me into the person I am today: a Hufflepuff with abandonment issues. I would start relationships then push people away, and after a while, away they went.

As I got older, I learned everything I needed to know about love through Aerosmith lyrics. Love was explosive, passionate and often dark. I lapped it up. I loved the drama.

My mum later remarried and soon along came my little brother Joe, followed by my younger sister Isobel. Growing up with two older brothers, I had longed for a sister to talk to and swap clothes with. My brothers used to run off and play Army, leaving me to play with my Barbie dolls on my own. They also used to bully me: a notable incident was when I opened up my Barbie suitcase to find a gigantic dog poo inside it. My mum made them clean it out but the smell never really went away. Neither did the trauma of being tied to a tree and left there all day. Mum only started to wonder where I was when it got dark, but at least it gave me time to grieve my poo-stained Cinderella Barbie.

Being a single mum with three kids was hard and money was tight. We lived in rented accommodation and I remember always being late for school, as our car never seemed to work. But we did have a massive garden and we were always outside. My brothers asked if they could dig a swimming pool, and to everyone's astonishment Mum said yes! So we had a huge hole in our garden for ever after that. Sometimes it would fill with rainwater and the boys would pretend it was a war bunker. I got nothing out of it, but it represented the hole of my despair. On reflection, maybe I should have fallen down it . . . I might have found more friends down there.

When my grandma was diagnosed with breast cancer she asked my mum if we would move in and look after her, and that's what we did. I was extremely close to my grandma and I adored everything about her grandma style. I loved that she went to bed early, drank Horlicks and watched soaps. I loved how she always believed in me and my dream to become an actress. She paid for me to go to Stagecoach and always encouraged me to perform. Before she died, she took us all to Florida to go to Disney World, which was a million miles from our usual holiday camping in muddy Cornwall. Another thing I loved about Grandma was her huge support of the Disney princesses, especially Pocahontas, who was my childhood favourite. Even as a child I had a genuine passion and concern for the environment . . . probably because my grandma was the human embodiment of Grandmother Willow.

We spent every Christmas and New Year – even the Millennium – at Grandma's house. She knew how to make Christmas so magical. When you walked in there was a huge talking Christmas tree called Douglas Fir. My cousins and I figured out that he worked on motion sensors, which provided hours of fun. One year I can remember Grandma pointing out the window, saying, 'Look! There's Santa looking for his reindeer!' And sure enough, there was Santa treading through the snow. (It certainly wasn't my father, LOL.) While we had our eyes glued to the window, someone rang the doorbell, and we ran to the door to find several large sacks of presents. Grandma's house was always so full of magic, and when Mum got remarried she held the reception there.

I have a huge family, and there were never enough chairs, but it was always so much fun. I would describe my ginormous, chaotic household as 'TA-DAH!' My family loves to drink, swear and show off. I believe that I'm a naturally loud talker because I constantly had to fight for the spotlight. Don't even get me started on Auntie Kate.

We lived with Grandma for a few years, then moved into the house my mum still calls home. It was still rented, it was a council house, but it was our house. There were seven of us under one roof, and we only had one bathroom, which didn't help the forever-late-to-school issue. Joe was born when I was nine, and I promptly dropped him on his head, but he turned out fine – although he was afraid of grass for the first few years. Isobel was born when I was thirteen, and although I was ecstatic to *finally* have a sister to share clothes with, her outfits ran a little small.

Home life was crazy with my two younger siblings, and when my eldest brother Tom went to serve in the Iraq War, I can't deny that I was mildly relieved to be upping my chances of getting early-access bathroom entry.

When I was fifteen I lied to Mum and told her I was sleeping at a friend's house, but instead went camping with a boy I'd met on a night out. It was incredibly dangerous and irresponsible. We were walking up a steep hill in pitch darkness in the middle of winter, and I was certain someone was shadowing us. I kept begging the boy I was with to turn on a light, insisting that we were being watched. He told me how silly I was, but turned on his phone torch and we both stopped dead. There was a man following us. (It wasn't my father.) I freaked out, remembering that absolutely no one in my family knew where I was. I was blonde and bisexual: I was going to die first. But after an awkward pause we just kept walking, leaving the scary man standing creepily in the dark. If you think I slept a wink that night, you are wrong. The boy ended up cheating on me, so overall it was a wasted night which fiercely contributed to my fear of the dark.

I regularly babysat my younger siblings, which caused my friends to joke that I sounded like a single mum when I'd say, 'Sorry, I can't come out, I have to look after the kids.'

As a teenager I was obsessed with Aerosmith. Steven Tyler was the drug-dependent father I never had, and I had posters of him, Britney Spears and Pamela Anderson all over my bedroom walls. I used to dye my hair all sorts of colours, which once backfired and turned my hair green. I had to wash it in ketchup every day until it returned to a shade on the right side of social acceptability. My teenage years were incredibly carefree. I loved cushions with tassels, intense sticks, sequins and people's attention. One time I ran around school in nothing but a towel.

What I Would Tell My Teenage Self

■ It's OK to like what you like.

■ Be yourself, unapologetically . . . unless yourself needs to apologise for something.

■ Think before you pluck.

■ Words hurt, so be kind, always.

■ People's opinions change. So don't stress too much if you can't educate someone. They will educate themselves if and when they are ready to grow.

■ Always try your best, no matter how exhausting it is. You can never regret what was once your best.

■ Don't let anyone tell you your dreams are silly. There's nothing silly about having goals and a strong focus.

I had some pretty wild nights when I was younger. My best friend and I used to joke that crazy things always seemed to happen to me, no matter how hard I tried to stay out of trouble. Like when I went to Download festival and my boyfriend set his legs on fire. Todd was absolutely crazy and I loved that about him. He was older than me, had long blonde hair and loved glam rock. He had a van, which was actually his dad's (my dad left and gave me nothing) and he drove it around fast and dangerously, blasting out music like Journey's 'Don't Stop Believing'. When he told me he was going to decorate the back of the van in leopard print I nearly fell in love. Tacky animal print is the way to my heart.

When we arrived at the festival Todd started unloading the van: wood, a generator and heaps of alcohol. We all set up our tents in a circle so we had our own little area in the middle to hang out in.

Most of my memories of the festival are blurry, but I remember I'd been away from our tents, and when I returned, Todd grabbed my hand and led me over to a patch of grass, and pointed at it proudly. I was like, 'What?' He had poured some flammable liquid on the ground to spell out 'I Love Rosie' and had set it on fire. Apparently this flammable liquid was supposed to keep burning but it had gone out, so the dramatic effect was visibly dimmed. Left behind were some frazzled patches of grass where an ostentatious and impulsive statement should have been. Much later that night I remember stumbling back to the tents after the final show, where I found Todd smoking. I watched as he threw his cigarette down at his feet. Todd was now on fire.

I kept my cool in this crisis. I grabbed a water bottle and started pouring liquid on him. A crowd started to gather, and I yelled at people to get help or to call the fire brigade. I reached for another bottle and poured it over the fire, which somehow seemed to aggravate the flames further. Our friend Mike yelled, 'THAT'S ALCOHOL!' A stranger from the crowd asked if he should piss on the fire. 'Yes, do it!' I screamed. 'Really?!' he replied, laughing, then proceeded to urinate. Todd had severe burns on his legs, but I wasn't that fussed, because, honestly, I didn't like him that much.

I was a person who made spontaneous decisions. During a particularly crazy, alcohol-induced game of hide-and-seek at my friend Gareth's flat, I climbed out of his window and into the window of another flat. Basically I broke in. I had no idea who lived there and didn't even stop to consider if they were home or not, I just adamantly wanted to win. As you can probably tell, I didn't think too much about the consequences of my actions, which is probably why I now over-analyse everything to an obsessive degree!

One person who shaped my teenage years was my first long-term boyfriend, Barney. Barney had bright carrot-orange hair, loved animals, and dressed like a painter-decorator. I loved him more than anyone I'd loved before. I spent every bit of spare time I had with him. We would go to his house after school, lie on his bed and talk. We talked so much we wouldn't eat dinner. His mum would offer us cups of tea or drinks and we'd just say no: we'd rather stay cocooned upstairs in his room. We were totally and utterly besotted with one another.

While my relationship with Barney developed, my relation-ship with my mum was breaking down. Another reason I spent so much time with him was to get away from home. Mum and I argued constantly. Most of the nights I did spend at home I would cry myself to sleep. Every moment spent together was tense and uncomfortable. Eventually, after a huge fight, I was forced to pack my bags, and I moved in with Barney.

After sixth form, Barney decided he wanted to travel to India. I was working at Lidl and had also just started a beauty therapy course, so I didn't have enough time or money to join him, so off he went, and I was left behind with his family. Now, don't get me wrong, his family were amazing, and I had an extra-special bond with his mum and sister. But living in their family home while Barney was away was something I found uncomfortable. More uncomfortable than the time I gave my first bikini wax to a real client and unwittingly glued her labia together (I was too liberal with the wax).

One afternoon I bumped into an old school friend, Sarah, and we got chatting. I told her about my current situation and she was sympathetic. We had a great catch-up before parting ways. A few hours later, she called me, totally ecstatic, and told me I could move in with her! Sarah's grandma had recently died, and she and one of her sisters had moved into her grandma's house, which had three bedrooms. The house now belonged to Sarah's auntie, and she'd said I could rent the third room. Call this coincidence or angelic assistance, but I moved in right away.

Sarah and I had been best friends since she'd joined my school in 2004. Her parents were also divorced, so after school we'd usually hang out at her dad's. (My dad wasn't around to hang out with.)

Sarah and her sisters were Mormons, which meant they didn't drink tea, coffee or alcohol, and didn't believe in sex before marriage, amongst a whole host of other doctrines. I would usually hang out with Sarah on a Saturday, sleep over and go with her to the Church of Jesus Christ of the Latter-Day Saints on a Sunday. Mormon church is different: first you have classes, like being at school, and then you have the service. It was about three hours long. Sometimes I found it really boring, sometimes I really enjoyed myself, and most of the time I was just plain hungry.

One thing I did enjoy about it was that I was always meeting new people, as the church would host Mormon missionaries, young men and women who were travelling abroad to teach people about the faith. One day, I met Elder Willhite, a handsome American missionary. Missionaries aren't even supposed to think about relationships of any kind, as their job is to embark on a spiritual mission to become closer to God and to bring others closer to God in turn. They even walk around in pairs, and aren't allowed to go anywhere unaccompanied by the other missionary. They have to be in bed by a certain time and can only listen to a certain type of music, all to keep them on the path of devotion to God. This was exactly what Elder Willhite was doing. Until I came along.

We saw each other as much as we possibly could, and in between we would talk on the phone, write letters and send tapes of our voices on Dictaphones. I wouldn't say I fell in love, but I'd say I was enamoured. Elder Willhite wanted to marry me, and with the 'no sex before marriage' rule, I could see why he wanted to rush things. He told me that his family were rich, that they had a huge house with a pool in Utah, and that we should get married and move in with them. In Mormon families things are very traditional: the women don't tend to work but stay at home and raise a family. Having zero presence from my own father and at the time and a strained relationship with my mum, moving in with a new family in Utah sounded tempting.

There was just one issue, and that was my bisexuality. I remember bringing it up with Sarah one day, and she told me that I would have to speak to the pastor. Being bi or gay was definitely frowned upon in the church. I can remember feeling extremely conflicted. I felt that there was no possible way I could change who I was, but I also felt a huge amount of guilt, shame and fear. I was genuinely uncertain as to whether God hated gay people and whether he'd allow me into heaven.

Elder Willhite got moved to another church. This happens often, as they rotate the missionaries around, but I suspect he was purposely moved away from me. Although we still kept in contact, him being further away, on top of my growing concerns, created a distance between me and the church. I started drinking tea again, then alcohol, and going out more with my other friends.

This created friction between me and Sarah, who was getting more and more heavily involved in the Mormon faith. She would go to parties with her church friends and would invite me along, but I would decline. She was always out doing something church-related, and we became like ships in the night, always just missing one another. Eventually, Sarah's sister came into my room and asked me to move out, for reasons that were never made clear to me. Reeling from the shock of it all, I was forced to get my own place, an idea that actually pleased me greatly, as I never wanted to rely on anyone else again.

I managed to rent a tiny flat above an Indian restaurant in St Johns, Worcester. It had three rooms: a bedroom, a bathroom, and a living room with a tiny corner kitchen. It cost £200 a month, water included, but that bargain came with another price: there was no central heating. The electricity ran off a meter, so instead of paying monthly I would have to top up every now and then. I figured out that I could get by on 50p a day (easy without any central heating!), and I tried to spend even less than that so I had some money spare, so I often spent my evenings in candlelight.

I finally began to feel like an adult. Despite having no internet, no TV and being constantly freezing, I was happy. I was self-sufficient and was finding my feet. For the first time in my life I felt extremely capable and independent, and I relished not having to rely on anyone else. I was moving forward and it was just me.

(My dad wasn't there.)

CHAPTER 2
OUR RELATIONSHIP

'Have you ever looked at your significant other and thought, *Not today . . . ?*'

ROSIE

Having our relationship unfold online is surreal. People have been watching us since our first dates, and have stayed to witness relationship milestones like moving in together, getting engaged, and eventually seeing footage of our wedding. Everything you see is candid and genuine. If we want to kiss and cuddle, we do, but if we don't, we don't. However, that doesn't stop a few people suggesting we fake our relationship for views! Even other YouTubers have told us they thought our marriage was only for the cameras, but I can assure you it's not.

Sometimes people ask me how Rose and I manage to live together and work together and still be so in love. I honestly find this concept baffling myself. We're together 24/7, from the moment we wake up to the moment we fall asleep, and we never run out of things to talk about. We still make each other laugh every day, I still catch myself being taken aback by how beautiful she is, and we still manage to surprise each other. The truth is, I don't know why it works so well, it just does. We're madly in love, and I don't take it for granted for a single second.

However, I'd like to mention that our relationship hasn't always been such smooth sailing. We met, we re-met, we argued, played games, tested each other and pushed each other away. I never imagined for a second that we would end up married and that our job would be sharing our lives with people on the internet. When I sit down and really think about it, I find it crazy.

Rose came into my life through a mutual friend. Are you ready for the twist . . . ? IT WAS THE LESBIAN I MET IN SCHOOL OUTSIDE THE MOBILE HISTORY BLOCK. We'll call her Blauren, as that's miles away from her actual name. Blauren and I went to school together, and I stayed on to attend sixth form while she went off to art college – where Rose was studying. Blauren showed Rose a picture of me while boasting about our flirtatious days in an attempt to impress her. It worked, but perhaps not in the way she had hoped. It's strange to write about how Rose was drawn to a photograph of me, but I just put that down to fate. I'm a big believer in all things happening for a reason, and Blauren showing Rose that picture set the wheels in motion . . .

ROSE

How awkward: I'd developed feelings for a piece of two-dimensional parchment. Let me contextualise this in order to defend myself. When I was at art college I met a girl who would soon become my first girlfriend. She definitely wasn't right for me, but she played an integral part in my life. (Rosie may have had history with her . . . but I had chemistry. LOLLLLLLLLLLLLLL.)

Blauren and I began our relationship the year after my traumatic bout of unrequited love with Bliv. My heart was almost healed, and Blauren was the exact opposite of everything I was usually attracted to. We were each other's first serious same-sex relationship, and that relationship, despite being incredibly unhealthy, lasted for four years and taught us both a lot. It taught *me* that sex in a Mini needs pre-planning and strategy, and that there was a strong possibility the girl of my dreams was Blauren's high-school fling. An awkward situation, I think you'll agree! Blauren made the fatal mistake of trying to impress me with tales of her high-school days and how she'd managed to seduce such an unattainably popular, wild and flirtatious bombshell, and she showed me a photograph of her to prove it. As soon as I saw the photo, I was obsessed. I was ABSOLUTELY obsessed. This was the biggest backfire in the history of flirtation, and one Blauren had *not* expected. From the way she'd described Rosie to me, I was totally invested in her story. A blonde brash bisexual who was dramatic, outspoken and constantly the centre of attention. Known for her seductive charm and flirtatious confidence, she was attainable yet somehow completely unattainable. This was exactly the kind of girl I was bound to fall for. She exuded sex appeal. When you looked into her eyes she captivated you. She got her thrills from people wanting her. And I wanted her.

Before Blauren and I officially embarked on our rollercoaster of a relationship together, I caught wind that Rosie was having a Halloween party, which I was extremely keen to get an invite to. Blauren made it her life's work to successfully block my advances, and she ruined my chances by telling Rosie that I was freakishly obsessed with the idea of her. YEAH, SHE WAS RIGHT, BUT THE HEART WANTS WHAT IT WANTS. Like I always say, stan hard or stay home. I never got my invite – not because Rosie thought badly of me, but because Blauren got her way and Rosie thought it was easier to avoid drama. I thought the best way forward was to attend inconspicuously. I bought the finest white sheet Matalan had to offer, cut two holes in it and there was my costume. The holes were for my eyes – just to make that categorically clear. I know this was a Rosie Spaughton party, but best not to assume its nature and dress appropriately.

Not only was I a ghost, but I was a ghost who didn't pay the entry charge. As there was a spirit already attending, and my face was covered, I managed to lie my way out of being one pound down: 'Oh, I've already paid, I'm the ghost from before,' I successfully conned Rosie's stepfather, a policeman by day, a FOOL by night (which is proof that I should pursue a life of polite petty crime).

When I saw Rosie dressed as the Queen of Hearts I felt starstruck. Like the time my mum clocked Alan Rickman being inconspicuous at the Hay Festival and boorishly announced his presence in the style of a town crier. I was so nervous to finally meet her. She was surrounded by boys. She left a visible trail of heartbreak everywhere she went, and, masochistically, I wanted to be next in line.

I asked my friend Square to introduce us. Her name was Square because she dated Nathan Square Head, whose head resembled a square. Intelligent reasoning. When Rosie and I were finally introduced I panicked because she didn't seem to have any time for me at all. She seemed standoffish, put out at having her trajectory towards boys obstructed. It was only when she realised that I was 'Blauren's Rose', the same Rose she was forbidden to meet, that her interest sparked and her eyes locked on mine. My soul was on fire, but that could have been indigestion from Korean barbecue. Never had anyone looked at me so piercingly, to the point where I couldn't hear anyone else in the room. She kissed my cheek and then she was gone. I was so in lust with this girl and I had no idea how to handle it.

ROSIE

Knowing Rose as well as I do today, turning up to a party uninvited and in disguise was incredibly brave and out of character for her. It's not the disguise that surprises me (Rose has a fierce interest in private investigation), but turning up to a party without knowing anyone is exactly the kind of social nightmare most people would want to avoid! I had a boyfriend at the time, but that didn't stop me feeling flattered by her attention and I enjoyed the lengths she went to to get to me.

ROSE

As time went by, Rosie fell off my radar. The obvious obsession I had with her put a heavy strain on my new relationship with Blauren. I wasn't allowed to talk about Rosie, let alone talk *to* her. Blauren went to great lengths to make sure we didn't ever see each other in person.

I was also acutely aware that I'd begun to idolise Rosie, a girl I had only met briefly and knew very little about. I was concerned at how strange that was, but knowing so few queer people in my area led me to think she was everything I wanted. Throughout my entire relationship with Blauren, Rosie would be at the back of my mind. Any excuse to talk about her to find out where she was and what she was up to. I felt so guilty thinking about another girl outside of the relationship I was in, but I should have recognised it earlier as an obvious indication of a bigger problem. I kept making excuses for myself: I thought it was just a case of 'the grass is always greener', and that I should never throw away something real for the idea of someone else. I'd never cheat on someone, but I also knew I was far too interested in Rosie to just ignore it.

On 7 December 2009 I went into Lidl, knowing Rosie would be working there. I took Blauren with me so I didn't feel so guilty. When we got to the checkout and saw Rosie, Blauren stormed off – but storming off and finding suitable sulking ground were just her brand, so it didn't feel particularly unusual.

Rosie saw her leave the store and gave me a look I'll never forget. She flirtatiously raised her eyebrows as if to suggest I had other options. (While writing this book Rosie has informed me that she raised her eyebrows to suggest I had a madam on my hands. I like my way better.)

A few years later my relationship with Blauren came to a natural end. I'd killed her. JUST KIDDING! In total honesty, Rosie had no bearing on my break-up, so fortunately my conscience was clear. Well, mostly.

ROSIE

While Rose was with Blauren I also started dating someone new, but Rose was always in the back of my mind. I can remember watching her early YouTube videos with my boyfriend and my next-door neighbour, saying how funny I thought she was, and staring at her photos on Facebook.

My boyfriend knew I was bisexual, and we had a discussion during which I told him, 'If we break up, I'm going to date girls!' I was thinking more and more about how I wanted to explore my bisexuality. I had dabbled with girls, but I'd never had a proper girlfriend. Eventually my boyfriend and I did break up, and although I was upset at the time, a part of me was excited to explore my options.

I had assumed Rose was totally off the market until I bumped into an old friend who told me that Rose and Blauren had split. I can remember exactly where I was at that moment, and I'm pretty sure I rushed home and messaged Rose straight away. I was desperate to get in there, because she and Blauren had had an on-again-off-again relationship, and I was convinced they would get back together. I just wanted Rose to give me a chance. I slid into her Twitter DMs and in my brazen style asked her out on a date with minimal small talk. Rose wrote back saying, 'Don't be naughty, you have a boyfriend!' I told her we'd broken up and we arranged to meet. I was ecstatic.

We had planned to go to the cinema on a Wednesday, but life had other ideas. On the Tuesday night I got locked out of my flat, and called my estate agent who came and bashed the door down like a true professional. I stayed up that entire night, guarding the hole where the door used to be, in case I got robbed or my cat escaped. So by Wednesday I wasn't in any fit state to go on a first date. I felt terrible about letting Rose down, and I later found out she had thought this was an elaborate excuse not to see her. It wasn't!

Still, we rearranged for the following week, and by the time it rolled around I was a bundle of mixed feelings. On the one hand,

I felt extremely confident. Rose had made it abundantly clear in the past that she was attracted to me, and I knew in my gut that we would get along great. But I started over-thinking things. What if we got along TOO well and it was more of a 'best friend' type vibe? What if there was no sexual chemistry? I wanted the date to go well, but I was also nervous of it developing into something serious. I wasn't as experienced with women as Rose was. I can specifically remember, during my pre-date shower, thinking that I had to treat my date with Rose exactly the same as I would treat a date with a boy. Still raw from my recent break-up, I was cautious of getting my feelings hurt. I decided that I would play it cool, and that I would be in control and would woo Rose, not the other way around. My barriers were safely up. But that didn't stop me texting her in a blind panic over what to wear on the date! When she texted back saying, 'OMG, I was just going to go sexy-casual!' I felt flooded with relief.

We met outside Vue at 8.30 p.m. on 20 October 2011. I arrived with a huge smile and cheap flowers (I was a student and it's the thought that counts). We got our tickets to see *Paranormal Activity 3*, but we were early, so headed to my local haunt where I bought us a gin and tonic each. I ended up drinking both of them – I needed a little Dutch courage.

I needn't have worried about a lack of chemistry. The heat between the two of us could have started a fire. (Good job Todd wasn't around.) I refused to let Rose pay for anything, partly because I wanted to charm her and partly because I wanted to have control. We sat huddled in a corner of the pub, chatting non-stop, only to be interrupted by a few of my friends who also happened to be there. My friend Anna took a photo of us, and that was it, our first date, cemented in history.

We went to the cinema where I bought a large sweet and salty popcorn, which we both ignored due to nerves, and for the duration of the film I clung on to Rose in both genuine and fake fear.

At the end of the evening I walked her back to her car. We stood looking at each other and I said, 'You're going to kiss me, aren't you?' Rose just leaned in, and that was our first kiss. A group of boys were walking past on the other side of the street and shouted, 'OH MY GOD, LOOK! LESBIANS!' but we were too engrossed in our own little bubble to care. We said our goodbyes and I walked away elated. It was probably the best first date I'd ever had.

ROSE

What do you mean 'probably'?! Wow, Rosie, don't over-commit or anything.

First of all, that popcorn tasted like ambiguous carpet findings, and the ratio of sweet to salty was disappointing. Second of all, that kiss was monumental, which is why I fist-pumped at the crescendo of a LeAnn Rimes classic as I drove away EUPHORIC.

I was so pleased with our first picture together. Not because Rosie was in it, but because I was working an off-the-shoulder jumper, complemented by a visible hanger string. A courageous look that screamed 'independent woman'.

Our first date went without a hitch, which surprises me because I'm usually the kind of girl who'd dislocate a joint and pretend she was fine. Or worse, sit in gum. Perhaps the universe thought it owed me, considering I was wearing corduroy trousers so was already at a disadvantage.

ROSIE

Our early dates were amazing. Rose and I shared the same sense of humour – she literally laughed me all the way to the bedroom. I loved the fact that being with Rose turned mundane activities like doing a food shop into the most fun, exciting time. We were both at university – me in my second year and Rose in her third – but we spent as much time as possible together. And when we did, it was electric.

All of our dates were incredible, even if we were just hanging around my flat watching films and getting drunk. Around the same time I started dating Rose, I bought myself a cocktail fountain, so we were constantly drinking lethal blue concoctions and falling about laughing. Another way we passed the time was going on a low-budget food adventure where we'd bought five items for £5 – which almost always ended up being onion rings and tinned curry containing questionable meat.

Our third date, at the Worcester Victorian Christmas Fayre, was my favourite. We didn't have much money but we went anyway and window-shopped, arms linked, walking around looking at the stalls. Then we went into TK Maxx and found the most random, hilarious pieces of furniture and promised to buy them all for our future home. Back outside in the cold night I spotted some mistletoe so we kissed underneath it, much to the shock and amusement of the people on the stalls nearby. Every date with Rose was so perfect it was like a scene from a movie or a dream.

Things I Love About Rose

■ Her work ethic. She works tirelessly to achieve her goals. Whatever she sets her mind to, she will achieve. Examples include graduating with her first-class honours and her interview with Camila Cabello!

■ Her perfectionism. She wants everything to be perfect and it usually is. I've seen her hit herself in the face when it's not.

■ Her love of *Buffy the Vampire Slayer*. There is nothing in this world so pure as when Rose discusses in detail the deeper meaning behind each episode.

■ Her emotional intelligence. Rose can read people like a book. Think you're hiding something from her? You're not. She can even tell what you're thinking right now . . .

■ How she plays *The Sims*. When Rose plays *The Sims* and throws her head back laughing I can't help but love her more.

As well as dating Rose, I was juggling university, work, and confronting my own sexuality. Although I had known from a young age that I was bisexual and was comfortable with that, some people now assumed that because I was dating Rose I had 'picked a side' and 'become a lesbian'. I can remember bumping into an old flame in a club and he said to me, 'Oh, hi, Rosie. I hear you're a lesbian now,' and it freaked me out. This was in the early days of Rose and I dating, and of course, back then I had no idea we'd end up married to each other! It was an uneasy feeling being mislabelled, and it honestly caused me a great deal of anxiety and stress. I worried that 'lesbian now' was my reputation for ever and that no boy would ever date me again. People's inability to accept that I could date both boys and girls added an unnecessary pressure to our relationship, and it was frustrating and panic-inducing. It knocked my confidence.

Our relationship wasn't without its difficulties. Rose could see that I had put emotional barriers in place to keep myself from getting hurt, and in an attempt to protect herself, she decided to play it cool too. She suggested we see other people, to make her appear less interested and perhaps to gauge my reaction. Having already been through a messy break-up, I was fearful about having an official relationship with Rose, in case history repeated itself and I'd have to endure another messy ending. I readily agreed to the no-strings-attached scenario Rose proposed – much to her internal dismay. We agreed to see other people, but to keep each other informed out of respect.

ROSE

I didn't understand why ON EARTH she'd interpret 'let's see other people' in a literal sense. Where was I losing her? My reverse psychology totally backfired, and had even worse results than my mum's first lip wax. But at least Mum could put ointment on her wounds; there was nothing I could apply to alleviate my jealousy.

Not being honest about how I felt led to ten months of game-playing, lying and tragedy in the style of Greek theatre. I absolutely loved it. Like any artiste, I was addicted to the pain. It felt great until it stung and then began to itch. My Spotify playlist 'Lesbian Jealousy' provided me with background music to an imaginary movie montage in which my character began to accept that her feelings were undeniably strong and that the games had to stop. So, with that in mind, I did what any self-respecting grown-up would do: I played even more games. I had a relationship with emotional turmoil like the one Millie Bobby Brown has with herself. I couldn't get enough. However, I was starting to question how successful the psychology behind my methods really was. I had assumed that making myself available for other people's courtship would immediately make me more desirable to Rosie. The truth was, I had few other options, whereas Rosie had a land force. I wasn't fazed. I would simply have to exaggerate my state of affairs. And by 'exaggerate' I mean 'fabricate'.

ROSIE

Naturally, as with all offers that are advertised as 'no strings attached', our relationship came with some complications. Rose would message other women in front of me, just to let me know she had options. We would both push each other away, just to see if the other one would chase after us. It was a desperate, passionate, crazy time – it was everything my hero Steven Tyler would sing about. Our relationship was teetering on love/hate.

I kept a diary but refused to write about Rose. Our relationship was so turbulent that I was convinced it would never work out (despite constantly going back for more), and was worried that people would see Rose as a 'phase'. I look back now and realise I couldn't write about Rose because I had internalised biphobia: I was almost ashamed about dating her.

Seeing no longevity in our relationship, I searched for what I already had with Rose with a man. And that's when I wrote about it in my diary.

ROSE

How was I to know that someone's diary wasn't appropriate passing-the-time reading material? I'm not proud of what happened next. It was catastrophic. One evening I was in Rosie's flat, alone, and there was her diary. 'Read me,' it said, in the voice of Lauren Jauregui.

I read it.

I can still feel the hot flush of shame and adrenaline. I couldn't stop. It was absolutely delicious. I read it from start to finish, and although I struggled deciphering her chicken-scratch handwriting, I got the general gist.

I WASN'T MENTIONED ONCE. Not even a footnote. Not even a pity mention, like at awards ceremonies when people thank the production staff. I wasn't deemed important enough to write about. That's how I interpreted it – like I was merely a guest star with a story arc orchestrated to get her to her heterosexual love interest in season 6. An LGBT character who was necessary for the protagonist's sexual awakening, but was killed off before it could amount to anything.

I read that Rosie had slept with a guy on a pool table while we were dating. She'd described it as the best sex she'd EVER had. How interesting that her diary was somewhere she'd happily lie to herself. Bitterness aside, I hated him. I wished him nothing but death by kangaroo rat, or by overplay of Simply Red. I'll never forget how much my heart hurt and how much I wanted to hurt her.

Things I Hate About Rosie

▓ When I told her she could see other people, she did.

▓ She loves to remind me of her dietary requirements.

▓ She takes the long route around a story by painting a picture with unnecessary information.

▓ She always asks me if I'm still listening, even when I've left the room.

▓ She takes baths even longer than her storytelling.

▓ She drops food on the floor on the first attempt at finding her mouth.

▓ She is dangerous to wake.

There were massive trust issues between us, and I was convinced that Rosie was seeing other people and not being honest with me. I was convinced because that was exactly what I'd just read.

As we all know, you should never read someone's diary: no good will come of it. Unless, of course, you can find the most incredibly psychotic way of tricking them into telling you the truth without having to admit to your own betrayal.

What was tricky was that I couldn't accuse her without revealing how I had discovered it, so I confronted her through a 'dream': I told her I'd had a psychic vision that she'd had sex with a ginger guy on a pool table, but that I knew that couldn't be true because obviously she would have told me. I knew she had too much respect for me to LIE . . .

Wow. I am a PIECE of work. Otherwise known as a genius. She said nothing all weekend, too scared to confess, and then told her mum I was psychic. My plan had worked.

'Bullshit,' said her mum. 'She's read your diary.'

Rosie sent me a text asking if I had read her diary, swiftly followed by one saying 'FUCK OFF AND DIE.' I also think she was trying to tell me something via the images she reblogged on Tumblr.

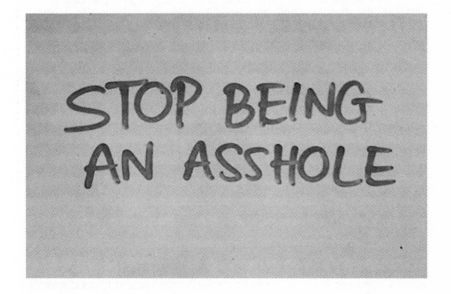

Tumblr post dated 12 April 2012

We didn't speak for an entire, agonising week, during which time Rosie took to Tumblr to expose my diary snooping and my parents encouraged me to renounce her on the grounds of her multiple betrayals. I also took to Tumblr. It was the only weapon at my disposal. I answered an anonymous question (which I can assure you I didn't send to myself):

What's the deal with you and Rosie?

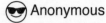 Anonymous

Peanut Butter loves Jam, but Jam isn't sure she wants to share the same sandwich any more ever since Peanut Butter read Jam's nutritional information without her knowing.

Peanut Butter feels terrible about what she did. She thought she was handling things smoothly, when really, the nuts were starting to appear. The trust Jam had in Peanut Butter was broken. But Peanut Butter's going to spend the rest of her shelf life mending the cracks in Jam's jar.

I tried to move on, convinced that Rosie couldn't handle a same-sex relationship and that my heart couldn't handle a further breaking.

The turning point was dramatic and involved Rosie texting me to ask for help getting her to the hospital. She was really poorly. It was a plea I couldn't ignore, even though my parents counselled against getting involved. I stayed with her throughout her time in hospital, and she says that was the point she fell in love with me. I had fallen in love with her months ago. (No offence, but get with the programme . . .) I'll never forget the way she looked at me when we were in A&E. Not because of her ugly mascara goop, but the desperation and sadness behind her eyes made me feel terrible for abusing her trust. Fortunately, there was a unique way to Rosie's heart. Not big displays of affection like you'd expect, or items of high material value, but chow mein. A classic Chinese dish of stir-fried egg noodles. I'm not saying it was going to fix everything (in fact it was probably going to lead to anticipated weight gain), but starch helped. Although it didn't remove the eye gunk I was beginning to focus on, but it wasn't the right time to bring that up.

Things I Love About Rosie

■ She looks like a pigeon.

■ You can always hear her in the event of an emergency.

■ She cries at tourist-board commercials.

■ That time I lost her at the airport only to find that she'd joined a queue and didn't know what it was for.

■ Her unique numbering system where eleven is 'onety-one'.

■ She doesn't let what others think affect her level of personal hygiene.

■ When she asks if I can take her on a shopping trip to Claire's Accessories (which I've never done and will never do).

Things I Hate About Rose

■ Her ability to win every argument by making me laugh whenever I try to make my point.

■ How she never takes me shopping at Claire's Accessories.

- How she refuses to let me have a princess net.

- How she purposely made the dog love her more than me.

- When I tell her something and then a few minutes later she repeats everything I've said back to me because she wasn't listening and now thinks it's her idea.

- How she loves telling me to hurry up even though she's far from ready.

- Whenever I'm ill she thinks I'm faking it.

- How her immediate response when I ask her to make me a drink is 'Fucking get it yourself!'

ROSIE

When I came out of hospital everything had changed. Rose and I began a serious monogamous relationship, and she had the most incredible, positive influence on my life. Although she's only two years older than me, her wisdom was beyond her years. Rose took the time to painstakingly chisel away at my impenetrable barriers, and, slowly but surely, I started letting her in. Rose's persistence was admirable: she would have one-way conversations with me, as I found it so difficult to open up. She was encouraging and inspiring, and seeing her working towards her goal of first-class honours spurred me to want more for myself. I loved her passion for her degree, and the way she made me feel like I had everything I needed within myself. With Rose's support, I started talking more, and, painfully slowly, I started to open up. As I did, so did she, talking to me about her OCD and the therapy she had had. Her stories of group therapy were hilarious, but the way her brain worked was almost exactly the same as mine. We connected spiritually, mentally and emotionally.

We dealt with some homophobic experiences together, but talking through my thoughts and feelings with Rose taught us both a bit more about bisexuality, and I began to feel more confident in myself. When we were stopped in the street by someone asking if we were lesbians because we were holding hands, Rose and I were strong enough to be able to laugh it off. And once I chased a guy down the road, shouting at him, furious because he'd seen us being together as an invitation. The first time we went to a nightclub together, the DJ stopped the music and just said 'Lesbians' into the microphone. We stopped kissing and looked around but couldn't see any.

I know I had a positive influence on Rose, too. She admired my independence, and I encouraged her to move out of her parents' house once she had left university. She ended up moving five houses down the road from my flat. We spent almost every night together, but it was good for Rose to have her own place, to pay her own bills and live life independently. We knew we would end up moving in together, but I'm glad we were sensible enough to make sure Rose got to experience living on her own.

ROSE

Loving each other and working together has been more successful than we ever dreamed. Never did I imagine that the dynamic of our explosive early days would lead to a partnership that works so well on so many different levels. In fear of sounding like a relationship snob, I think the key for us has been communication. I communicate by throwing things and Rosie communicates by avoiding the objects. It works. Communication is everything. We're so close now that we can even tell what the other is thinking. Perhaps it's easier for me to be telepathic because I crudely read the chronicles of her inner monologue, but say what you will, it's an artful way to converse. Having patience is another integral factor to a successful relationship. I patiently wait until she's finished talking and it's my turn to speak. I'm actually still waiting . . . I've really developed this skill.

Perhaps this is why so many people assume we're related before they assume we're together. Our chemistry confuses people, and watching as they try to work out the dynamic of our relationship can be both entertaining and tiresome. They will list every possible option before the idea that we might be a couple springs to mind. But what's even more infuriating is the fact that they feel like they need to ask. Every Uber driver I've ever had has questioned why they were taking us back to the same house. The interrogation is so uncomfortable that it often makes me choose walking for forty minutes over the convenience of being driven.

If we were two men I find it hard to believe we'd be asked the question: 'Are you brothers or just friends?' Why probe? What does it matter? It's actually a little intimidating, and it's something I could really do without. I constantly feel pressured to give a detailed account of how Rosie and I met, what we do for a living, and why we live and work at the same address. There have even been countless occasions when I've felt threatened, and, sickeningly, have felt forced to give false answers to protect my own safety.

But the world is changing positively and people are becoming wiser. The acceptance of love as equal and impossible to measure for comparison is happening all over the world. When I was younger I used to scoff at those who thought love alone could conquer the destruction hatred could bring. That was until I learned that killing someone with kindness is always more effective than attempting to cause them pain. I know because I've been on the receiving end of it! But until the day the world becomes entirely tolerant and informed, we must endure the repetitive ignorance of the following . . .

Stupid Questions We've Been Asked

All the below are questions we have been asked by genuinely well-intentioned yet dumb AF people.

◼ 'Are you sisters or friends?'

◼ 'You've got a room booked with a double bed – would you prefer two singles?'

◼ 'Aren't you too pretty to be gay?'

◼ 'Who's the man?'

◼ 'Do you miss men?'

◼ 'What's your husband's name?'

◼ 'How do you . . . do it?'

◼ 'Where do you meet gay people?'

◼ 'Are you twins?'

◼ 'Bisexuals are just greedy, aren't they?'

◼ 'Don't you think you just haven't met the right man?'

And the best one I've ever heard, while shopping for wedding rings:

◼ 'If you both buy those rings and wear them on that finger won't they look like wedding rings?!'

ROSIE

It sounds offensive when I say that I never, ever imagined that I would end up marrying a woman. What I *mean* to say is that I couldn't imagine it because I never thought it was even an option. I didn't know any woman who was married to another woman in real, adult life. I can't point to my own house on a map, let alone Brighton. How would I know there was a gay capital of England when I once thought London was on the coast?

I knew my attraction to women was strong, but I believed it was inevitable I would settle down with a man eventually. But what life taught me is that it doesn't always care for your plans.

When Rose and I go out for dinner or coffee, we're fascinated by the number of couples who don't talk to each other. Partly because I could have a conversation with a shower curtain, but also because we always have so much to say to each other! And when you think about how much time we spend together, it's almost unbelievable we still have things to talk about.

We go from discussing our deep, psychological inner workings that stem from our childhoods to writing low grade kitchen hip-hop. We have ugly, greasy days when we sit and work furiously, and we have days when we dress up to impress each other. Sometimes it might seem like a mundane day, but if I had to spend it without her, I'd hate it. In fact, whenever we do spend time apart I always plan ahead, making sure to cram my time with activities so I don't spend it missing her. Gross.

It's cringey to talk about our love; I'm aware that we're still young, and I certainly don't want to lecture anyone. There are people who have spent fifty years married to each other, and God, I want that to be us one day. I want to grow old with her, even though the idea of old-person smell and crusty excess skin repulses me.

ROSE

Rosie and I didn't even consider marriage in our future until I collapsed down the station steps running to catch a train for an event we were appearing at. I was out cold and Rosie was screaming for help. She wasn't allowed to accompany me in the ambulance because she wasn't a family member or next of kin. She had to bravely call my parents, who were still incredibly wary of her, to break the news that I was being rushed to hospital, and then she had to stand back and let other loved ones take her place.

Luckily, I was OK, just a dangerous mix of dehydration, low blood pressure and unmeasurable talent, but the shock for both of us was traumatic. A month later, I proposed to Rosie on her twenty-fourth birthday with a hand-illustrated drawing and an antique ring. I asked my best friend, Emma, a children's book illustrator, to draw me proposing to Rosie, so that it was something she could physically unwrap. This mastermind plan avoided her guessing it was going to happen, and the picture serves as a constant reminder of the days I used to be romantically spontaneous.

Our wedding was so beautiful, full of love and family acceptance. We had come a long way from our early days of mistrust, mess and mistakes. I think somewhere, subconsciously, we both knew this was where we would end up, but neither of us had a clue how to make it happen.

ROSE & ROSIE – MRS & MRS

If one of you wants to do something and the other doesn't, how do you compromise?
Rose: Compromise is far easier to achieve when you give in. Communication is key in any relationship, and communicating that I am listening has been a big learning curve for me, and it's revolutionised any potential dispute. Whenever I used to argue with Rosie, it was because I wasn't listening to her opinion properly, not because I disagreed with it.
Rosie: We have a discussion, and we will usually understand each other's viewpoint. Then we will compromise. But normally Rose and I think the same way and want to do the same things, so this situation is actually very rare!

Who is generally more right?
Rose: A complex question. We both have areas of expertise. I'm very strong at being able to spot red flags when it comes to any business decisions, and Rosie is always right when it comes to outfit choices. Outfits are everything. Trust me, I know: I had a brief but unforgivable poncho phase. In all honesty, I'd say we both make good decisions after having learned from every bad one we've ever made . . . such as marriage. (Obviously joking.)
Rosie: Annoyingly, Rose is. But I'm not too far behind.

What would be the one thing to break you up?
Rose: When Rosie puts empty cartons in the sink and thinks they'll wash themselves up. They float on the greasy film of dirty washing-up water when they could have just been rinsed out and put in the recycling. We've spoken about it in

the past which has led to a compromise: she will continue to do it and I shall allow it.

Rosie: I don't even want to think about it.

Do you ever get bored of each other?

Rose: Never. We have such exciting lives it feels like we're always on a new adventure! But take all that away and we'd still never get bored. Rosie and I are very lucky to be married to each other and also to like each other. We laugh over the lamest, most ridiculous things, and even when times are tough we manage to trivialise it by joking and messing around. We never have time to get bored of each other because every day is so different! But one thing I will say is that hearing about her struggle of trying to grow in her eyebrows is getting really boring . . .

Rosie: Never.

Do you ever argue about politics?

Rose: Not really! We actually have the same opinions: it's my opinion that I'm the fan favourite and Rosie agrees. But when it comes to serious politics, we rarely discuss it. Not in fear of having an argument, but because we try to shut out negativity from our lives. Unavoidable at times, but we're extremely focused on trying to change the world for the good, by bringing light to our current political climate, and by being happy!

Rosie: Sometimes, but very rarely. We are generally on the same wavelength!

What is the one gift you wish you could give each other?

Rose: I'd love to give Rosie the gift of volume control. But in all honesty, I would love to be able to rid her of her food allergies. Although it's funny to see her blow up like a beach ball, I've been told that it's actually not funny. Material possessions don't mean much to us, and there's not one particular thing that I want, other than a modest house with an adult adventure playground.

Rosie: Hmmmm, that's a tough one. I would give myself the gift of waking up early, because Rose hates having to drag me out of bed every morning. Then perhaps she'd get the gift of breakfast in bed!

What is your favourite physical part?

Rose: Her spleen. Looks great from every angle.

Rosie: I love every part of Rose equally, but I really love it when she pulls silly faces!

How do you cope with each other's mental health issues?

Rose: This can be tough. Sometimes Rosie will remember an embarrassing memory and will shout, 'Ahhhhhhhh!' in an acute cringe spasm. If this happens while I'm driving, her flustered shrieks of anguish make me think I've flattened a box of orphaned fast-lane puppies, and I slam on the brakes in a cold-sweated panic.

Rosie: One thing I did when Rose and first I got together was read a book about OCD. It helped me understand the way she thinks as well as her viewpoint. Also, since we've been together I have become a LOT tidier! I used to be an extremely mucky pup. Now I want the house to be as clean as my conscience. I don't think her mental health has ever been an issue in our relationship. I love Rose for exactly who she is, and I wouldn't have her any other way.

What annoys you most about each other?

Rose: Rosie's inability to enjoy food without eating with it her mouth open. When she's devouring something she particularly likes her lips refuse to touch, and she makes this squelchy noise like an obnoxious cartoon character. It makes me want to throw things.

Rosie: Rose doesn't look for things properly and it infuriates me! She'll ask where something is and it's right in front of her. She'll ask if I've borrowed her make-up when it's right there in her own make-up bag and she hasn't even looked for it yet. It drives me absolutely mad! USE YOUR EYES! LOOK! If she asks me where something is, I'll reply with really clear directions, like, 'The white set of drawers in the bedroom, top drawer,' and she'll say, 'Where? Which room? Did you say it was in a drawer? I can't see it.' And she'll be in the wrong room looking in the wrong drawers. It honestly works me up so much I froth at the mouth.

When making big life/work decisions, who generally makes the final decision?

Rose: Let me tell you an analogy a good friend (a friend I actually like) once made. In her relationship, and in mine and Rosie's, there is a shop manager and a shop owner. Rosie is the shop manager, responsible for the day-to-day running of our business and I, as shop owner, usually make the final call on any big decisions. But everything is discussed at length. It's going to be mega awks if I have to fire her though . . .

I might delegate that job to Rosie, considering it probably falls within her remit.

Rosie: We would never go ahead with a big life or work decision unless we were both 100 per cent confident about it. We'd never let just one of us call the shots. Even if we have to discuss something a million times, we'll eventually agree on what to do, then go ahead with it together.

If you could change one thing about each other what would it be?

Rose: When she says 'give it me' instead of 'give it to me'. xGrammatically incorrect use of language is worse than cheating.

Rosie: I would try to relieve Rose of her worries. With her OCD, she is always thinking and analysing, and she finds it very hard to switch off, especially at night. Sometimes I fall asleep and she stays up stressing, and I really hate that. I would love a remote control so I could turn off her work mode and help her relax a little more.

Who would you allow each other to have a celebrity snog with?

Rose: As long as I'm allowed to kiss Camila Cabello, Rosie can do anything/anyone she likes. Just as long as if she's cheating, she's cheating with grammatical correctness.

Rosie: Camila Cabello for Rose. Definitely James McAvoy for me!

What film/book have you made each other watch/ read because it was seminal for you and did she get it?

Rose: *Good Will Hunting*. Robin Williams reminds me a lot of my father, and his calmness and wisdom in that film reminded me of how Dad dealt with me when I was a troubled mathematical genius with a centre parting. Rosie loved it, despite her complaints that Minnie Driver had a head so large it couldn't be taken seriously.

Rosie: Rose and I both got obsessed with *Room*. I read the book and we both watched the film three times. It's about a woman who was kidnapped and held hostage and has a child in captivity. It sounds so dark, and it is, but the message behind it is to appreciate life, even the tiny, trivial things, and we both fell in love with that.

What is the biggest thing you argue about?

Rose: I don't take my empty cup downstairs after I've had my morning coffee in bed, and that seems to greatly irritate Rosie. Now that she's mentioned it a few times, I go out of my way never to bring it downstairs, because I'm THAT person. But if she picked up the Hoover once in a while perhaps I'd stop being such an arsehole.

Rosie: We never argue! We occasionally bicker about stupid things, but we never argue.

Who takes longer to get ready?

Rose: I take longer to do my make-up and Rosie takes longer on her outfit choice!

Rosie: Rose does, but she always starts to get ready before me while I procrastinate, so we usually end up timing it perfectly!

What would she say if someone told her to 'get a proper job'?

Rose: She'd laugh. And then do her go-to exasperated exhale, which translates as 'Twat.'

Rosie: Rose is quite assertive and wouldn't let anyone put her down. She would perfectly put them in their place.

How would she deal with predatory behaviour?
Rose: I'm only predatory when she's eating food I want, although you're probably talking about other people's behaviour . . . Well, I would deal with it by punching the guy in the throat, and Rosie would lock her teeth around their ankles like a bear trap until she reached cartilage.
Rosie: Oh, Rose has dealt with this many times before. One time she finished a guy off with her words and then I threw a packet of Jacob's crackers at his Adam's apple.

Who is prettier?
Rose: I read this as 'pettier', so me.
Rosie: Hmmm. I find it hard to compare us because we look so different. I'm short, she's tall, she's dark-haired, I'm fair, etc. I think we each have our own strengths, but overall I'd say Rose. Or possibly me.

What is a romance killer?
Rose: Unidentified smells.
Rosie: Rose will poo with the door open and give me a running commentary. I will go to a far-away bathroom, shut the door, and play music very loudly. But I like that she's so comfortable around me.

Do you have nicknames for each other?
Rose: Normally she goes by Subby, for 'subordinate', but I also call her Wony. I can't even remember where that came from!
Rosie: We call each other Wony and Bony, it's absolutely disgusting. It doesn't matter who's who, because we

switch it around. We each have a baby voice that we use on the other when we want something, and so far it's always worked like a charm.

Who is the funniest?
Rose: Me. I mean neither of us. We bounce off each other's energy and laugh with and at each other! One thing I love about Rosie is her ability to laugh at herself. Her brain works wonderfully, her thought process is so unusual and unique – it's the funniest thing in the world to me! As soon as you take yourself too seriously you've become divorced from your audience – and it means life is far less fun!

Rosie: Rose is more consistently funny all day, every day. But I like to think that I occasionally come up with some absolute classics which we then use as long-running jokes. Something Rose and I also love to do is pronounce things wrong on purpose, because we think it's hilarious. We do it all the time, and if someone listened in they probably wouldn't be able to understand us. It's like our own language.

What three words would you use to describe each other?
Rose: Selfless, loyal, pure.
Rosie: Silly, witty, intelligent.

Who is the better cook?
Rose: I have a few signature dishes! I make a mean sweet-chilli salmon with rice noodles. Rosie could cook if she wanted to, but she'd rather wash up and then place empty cartons on the dirty washing-up water. I'm fine with it.

Rosie: Rose is! I don't do much cooking any more these days, I leave it up to Rose. But I do do more dog-walking, so I think it all balances out.

What item of each other's clothing would you put on the bonfire?

Rose: Her late-night dog-walking ensemble. Let me itemise it: a winter coat worn over a dressing gown, pyjama bottoms, black dolly shoes, a scarf, complemented by an ambiguous if not downright confusing hairstyle I refer to as a nest.

Rosie: I don't hate any of Rose's clothes! If anything, I want to steal them all. We do share clothes, but I'm petite, so everything I borrow of Rose's is a little too long. I think there might be loads of things I wear that she would love to burn.

Who has the sunniest outlook on life, and is that annoying?!

Rose: Rosie is the most positive person I've ever met in my life. I am never allowed to wallow in my own angst. Sometimes that's annoying, when I just want to listen to Dido and repost vague lyrics on Tumblr. But I'm so thankful for her, because whenever I've reached my snapping point she's always there to balance me out.

Rosie: That would be me. I'm an optimist and Rose is a realist! I think sometimes it annoys her, but I get equally annoyed whenever she expects a negative outcome from something. I always try to be positive!

Who is the most creative?

Rose: Rosie is fantastic at generating ideas, especially under pressure, and I love bringing them to life! We both get so excited at the idea of starting new projects, and neither of us could ever do a job that wasn't creative.

Rosie: I think that would be me. I'm good at thinking up unusual ideas, and time pressure doesn't really phase me. I think things up and Rose helps me bring them to life!

How do you deal with offline homophobia?

Rose: I honestly pity those who make it their life's work to shit on other people's happiness. What a total waste of time and energy. In the majority of cases, it's down to ignorance and lack of education. That doesn't make it any less tiresome to have to deal with, but I find that a nice, calm, belittling response usually shuts them down. There's not much they can do when they've been outsmarted. But my advice would be to never argue with an idiot: as the saying goes, 'they will drag you down to their level and beat you with experience'.

Rosie: We do occasionally receive homophobic reactions from strangers. Rose and I are both quite outspoken, so unless the situation was particularly dangerous, we would probably call them out on it.

Do you ever get jealous?

Rose: Yes. I get incredibly jealous and it's a trait that I wish I didn't possess. Jealousy is such a horrid feeling to endure. On the one hand it's crippling, but sometimes it reminds you of what you want. I suffer from various types of jealousy. Relationship jealousy, when someone is clearly attracted to my wife and I'm like, 'Aww, how cute ... Leave.' Then there's backwards jealousy, when someone takes a fondness to Rosie and I'm like, 'HI. WHY AM I NOT ATTRACTIVE TO YOU?' And then there's professional jealousy, which can be a fantastic motivator to get us to where we want to be.

Rosie: Yes, but I think sometimes a bit of jealousy in a relationship is healthy. But neither of us has ever been so jealous it has seriously affected our relationship.

Is there something you get her to do because you think it is good for her?

Rose: Wash. But also make sure she listens to another person's perspective before reacting emotionally.

Rosie: A lot of things! In our career I have often pushed Rose to do things she hasn't been comfortable with, and I can honestly say that now she can do a lot of things that were outside her comfort zone. Rose's nerves used to get the better of her, but I forced her into situations she didn't always like, and now I feel she has totally conquered a lot of her fears. She also does that herself with her fear of flying! She refuses to let it stop her from travelling.

If only one of you could bear children, who would it be and why?

Rose: I know I'm going to make a great parent regardless of whether the child is biologically mine or Rosie's. I'm not like a regular mum, I'm a cool mum. Having said that, I know I'm a going to do all the things I criticised my own mother for doing, because, as an adult, I understand that when you love your children all you want is the very best for them. So bribery all round, am I right?!

Rosie: Maybe me, because I'm slightly more fearless. But that's a tough one. I think we will both be great mothers but for different reasons.

If you weren't YouTubing together, what other career could you do as a couple?

Rose: Private investigators.

Rosie: Presenting. Like Richard and Judy, only with four breasts and without the wardrobe malfunction.

'Hi guys, and welcome to the internet!'

ROSE

Throughout my childhood years I always wanted to be an actress. I remember standing in front of my grandparents at the indistinguishable age of 'bowl fringe', ready to perform covers of *Sister Act* choir numbers as a solo artist. I loved commanding the room in my Minnie Mouse knitwear, and the hit of adrenaline was better than the rush I got from petting someone else's dog. For as long as I can remember, being in front of an audience was exactly where I wanted to be. But it was my progressive performance as a Wise Man in the primary-school Christmas nativity that was worthy of an IMDB credit.

As a child of the eighties, it was a real privilege for me to own a camcorder. Unfortunately, our family's finances had taken a hard hit the summer we went to Universal Studios where my brother insisted on buying a replica of the DeLorean from *Back to the Future*. As a result, we had to make do with disposable cameras and a diet of bread and milk. But by the age of seventeen I'd saved up enough money to buy myself a MiniDV camcorder, which allowed me to capture fly-on-the-wall family-holiday gold – mostly footage of my brother's teenage tantrums, which easily could have featured on trash terrestrial television if only I'd known the right people. Dramatic mouth zoom-ins were my favourite artistic practice, but seemed to anger my subjects greatly. The most climactic day of shooting was in Cornwall, when John's request for an LED light painting was rejected by my father and my passion to capture the moment on camera was forcefully opposed by all. But no documentary filmmaker ever got famous by not doing!

I saw this as my biggest challenge so far. Undercover filming required patience, skill and finesse. I had none of these things. But what I did have was an obnoxious desire to intrude on people's personal space, three blank tapes, and a category-5 tantrum on the brink of impact – and I wanted to be in the eye of the storm. However, we lost John in the Lost Gardens of Heligan. His sulk stank, it fogged up my lens and he lost me at the rhododendrons. An hour and a half later he re-emerged, and our family plan to act like we hadn't noticed he was gone was in full swing. During John's dramatic disappearance I'd been advised by my father not to antagonise people with my camera and further contribute to an already turbulent climate. I'd explained that quality content could only be achieved when there were several risk factors. (For example, the short documentary I made about my mother's bunion. I asked the questions that counted, such as, 'Mum, do you always turn to McCoy's beef and onion crisps when you're upset about your bunion?' I was told to switch off the camera and leave the room, so I took that as a yes.)

Documenting important moments in time excites me to this day. It was never a short-term trend, and having creative control of my own work led me to study film at degree level. My mum worked full-time purely to put us kids through university – and also to fill the monetary void left by the DeLorean. I am eternally grateful for my mum's dedication to our education, and I feel like she's made amends for the time she put ink erasers in our Christmas stockings. I was told that breaking into the film industry would rely entirely on who you knew rather than on your own merit. Highly encouraging. It seemed that neither *Bunion, Heligan Storm,* nor even the gritty nature of my later work, a factual piece documenting my sister's Herculean toilet deposit and its refusal to vacate her studio flat, could guarantee a break.

In my opinion, my show reel was strong. Filming my brother in one of his sulks was becoming my passion project. Seeing if I could evade the explosion of aggression when he noticed he was being filmed was a thrill I cannot describe. Angering John not only pleased me as a human, but it was my calling. It resulted in content that would have gone viral if only YouTube had existed at the time. The interplay between close-ups of my fuming brother's furrowed brow and my mum's expression of passionate distain was riveting, it was honest, it was silver-screen excellence.

Capturing their strenuous relationship and turning it into comedy made life much easier to deal with, and that concept lies at the heart of our YouTube channel. Life online is exactly that: it's life. Life can be a real piece of shit, but it's the way we talk about these things that makes them far easier to manage. It's not downplaying the stresses of life, but breaking them down and wrapping them up in a positivity blanket. Who else just vommed? Perhaps 'positivity blanket' was a little *extra* (Generation Z power-phrase bonus!!), but I'm a firm believer in the power of positivity, and uplifting our audience is our main goal. That, and all the money YouTube brings.

To the bemusement of most tabloid journalists, traditional media is becoming obsolete. The pleasure I get from reading belittling articles about YouTubers powered by confusion and resentment nearly tops the pleasure I get from watching people's Tube tickets not working and the embarrassment that follows when the barrier won't open.

YouTube has given people the opportunity to become online personalities and stars within their own right, but for a long time this wasn't apparent to me, even in 2012 as I was graduating top of my class. There were two other students in my year who also got first-class honours. There were actually only two other students in my year full stop, so technically we were *all* top of our class. But as a YouTuber I like to embellish a story, and title it 'I Graduated Top of My Class Then Died (Not Clickbait!).'

Throughout university my appreciation of YouTube as a platform was minimal. Back then it wasn't seen as a way of making money, let alone a career path. It was used primarily for cat compilations and by indie-pop bands. But it was a platform that allowed anyone to upload their creations to a worldwide audience, and the thought of that excited me. What infuriated me the most about the world of post-university employment was that you needed a certain level of industry experience to be regarded as competent within your desired field. That begs three questions. The first: Is anyone truly competent within their field? The second: How does one *gain* experience when you're thwarted by not having *enough* experience? And the third: Why did my mother tell me I needed a degree to become anything I wanted to be? I've never seen a mime artist with a student loan. Their only job requirement is to think outside the box.

I'd always felt that I was meant to entertain people, ever since my live stage adaption of *Forest Gump* (a long afternoon for my family, as I played every character, but I generously provided biscuits during Act 12). I relished the opportunity to expose myself, and saw that my degree module in Online Content was the perfect opportunity to make my YouTube debut. The requirement for the module was to 'produce a viral video'. Simple. Points for a spirited and ambitious curriculum! Hats off to Hereford College of Arts for an achievable breakdown of requirements.

Fortunately, with the one measly hour a week of one-to-one time with my tutor, I had all the support I needed. The rest of the week was branded 'independent study', so I did just that. I independently studied the ways I could earn as much as my tutors were earning for even less effort. I know I sound like a resentful tabloid journalist, so I'll briefly digress . . . I graduated university with first-class honours, and while embarking on post-graduation employment I discovered that this accolade was not recognised by Pizza Express. The hurt cut deeply. Deeper than the flimsy *authentic* Italian pizza base considered more sophisticated than deep-pan. Pizza politics aside, the reality that I wasn't deemed qualified enough to bring other people their Sloppy Giuseppes hit me harder than an M. Night Shyamalan narrative twist. At the same time there's my university tutor, who got paid a very respectable wage for turning up just once a week with tales of how she dropped her tobacco in the toilet but picked it out and smoked it anyway. Hideous. She also once dropped a baguette, picked the salad up off the carpet, shoved it back in the bread, and was shameless enough to eat it in front of my face. And don't get me started on how much YouTubers earn. LOL.

Anywho, it was my parody version of Ke$ha's 'TiK ToK' video that propelled me to mediocre levels of internet stardom. I was genuinely shocked that a video filmed in such low quality garnered so much attention. My peers were getting between 40 and 60 views on their module submissions, while I managed to get 16,000 in just a few days. I'm certainly not one to blow my own trumpet (if anything, I'd blow a flugelhorn, because that seems like a sensible jump in millennial fashion), but I was quietly smug.

I suppose the question that most people want to know the answer to is 'Are you rich?' The truth is, I'm rich in a number of things: insecurity, wit, acne scars and the odd mental health disorder, but most importantly, money. I jest, but like any other career, you get out of it what you're willing to put in. I understand the fascination most people have when it comes to YouTube earnings, but that doesn't mean I enjoy answering their questions. Never in my right mind would I ask someone, 'What kind of money do you make from that?' And never have I answered that question. (Apart from when I legally had to at the US embassy, while Rosie was down the hall vomiting, but that's a colourful story for another day.)

The point is, it's either jealousy or lack of social intelligence that leads people to believe it's acceptable to pry. So I'm going to clear up a few things. Yes, it's possible to make millions from YouTube. No, I haven't done that yet. Yes, brand deals are the bulk of our earnings. No, I would never advocate something I didn't believe in. Yes,

I'm actually married. No, I'm not gay for pay. Yes, I have a 'back-up plan': it's called 'not failing at my original plan'. No, I wouldn't exploit my children for views; I'd exploit them for the money I made from views. Yes, YouTube is just as hard as any other career. No, it's not just making one video a week.

My biggest grievance is the idea that being a YouTuber is easy and that anyone could do it. Well, anyone can! So I suggest to those who seem agitated by the success of online influencers to go out and do it themselves. If it's that easy, go and grab it with two hands and let's all reap the rewards and celebrate our book deals in #Mykonos! (Only hardcore internet fans would appreciate that Mykonos reference. It seems it's a popular sponsored destination for YouTubers to travel to, and I'm aware my sarcasm level just peaked to a record high.)

Like most jobs, people assume that if you look the part, you can fulfil the role. (If that were true, Donald Trump would make an excellent mop head, but no one wants pugnacious Republican mildew smeared across their rustic wooden floors. That's not even suitable for floors with a low-cost 'wood effect'.) But what does it mean to be a YouTuber? I can understand why for some influencers money can become a driving force, because it's the same in any career and is totally down to the individual. But I can honestly say that my and Rosie's top priority is our relationship, closely followed by creating a happy place for people to escape to online.

After the success of my Ke$ha parody I continued YouTube strictly as a hobby. It was a free platform for people to be creative, which is why I believe Rosie and I started making videos for the right reasons, before being 'YouTube famous' was even a term. We started out with the sole intention of having entertaining conversations about everything and nothing, which other people could check into. We wanted to create a place that allowed them to have five minutes when the stresses of life were forgotten. I needed that myself, so I knew it was something that could benefit others. It was also nice just to document the time we spent with each other, and, naively, I never thought that my and Rosie's romantic relationship would become the prime focus of our channel. It seemed our onscreen romance was what garnered most people's attention, yet surprisingly that didn't put any pressure on our relationship, as you might assume it would.

I always thought the best way to normalise same-sex relationships was just to be visible, and not necessarily to shape your content around LGBT activism. Comedy was my passion, and being gay was simply an aspect of me, so I never pictured it defining our videos, just like it hasn't defined me as a person. Perhaps I didn't realise how much people needed representation. In my mind, being gay was such a non-issue that it didn't need to be defended, only celebrated, through just being ourselves. In many ways I think this is why we became popular: we weren't militant, we weren't preachy, we were just being ourselves. Not that there's anything wrong with being an activist and consciously raising awareness of equal rights – it's admirable and is certainly necessary – but at the time, being gay just wasn't what I wanted to repeatedly talk about.

Our relationship evolved publicly, and with every video we made we got closer and closer, and our audience started to get bigger. But we weren't aware of the numbers, let alone tracking our growth or being conscious of the opportunities it could bring. We didn't have a game plan or a regular upload schedule; what we did have was unforgiving lighting and too much space between our eyebrows. Rosie's eyebrows didn't even match and embodied the shape of punctuation.

When people ask me, 'What's the secret to a successful YouTube channel?' I always tell them to be passionate. If you have something to say, say it with passion. Never be anyone other than yourself, because viewers are smart: never underestimate their ability to see through an act. Contrived, copycat content has a short shelf life, and desperation for fame is easily recognised. Don't try to be polished – be honest. How many viral videos have you seen with a high level of production value? Few, because raw, honest content is what people subscribe for. That and boobs.

One of the biggest challenges I've had as a YouTuber is people assuming I'm only successful because I've been lucky. I actually quite enjoy being spoken to like I'm some arrogant, deluded thicko who doesn't understand what it's like to work an ordinary 9 to 5. Even if that were true and I'd never had a 'real job', what's 'lucky' about building and retaining a loyal community of online viewers hingeing solely on your personality? Being a YouTuber doesn't make you better or luckier than others; it makes you an easy target for jealous people who don't understand how it works.

'What are you going to do when it's all over?' they ask, with that feigned expression of concern as if it's your welfare they care for. Their knowledge of the platform is so little that it's easier for them to pretend that your success is too confusing to understand rather than congratulate you. I absolutely salivate at the idea of destroying someone like this with passive aggression. I believe it to be something of an art, and the more successful we've become online, the more I've had to deal with a particular breed of human. Let me elaborate.

The City Serpent. A creature of great strength and professional prowess. Aggressively fast-paced, stealthily discreet, psychoanalytical, commercially astute, but above all else, one step ahead, always. You'll usually find serpents nesting in and around the city, but before I tell you how to spot one, let me first explain how they've come to exist and why they thrive. In a competitive young professional climate, whether it's YouTube or an office environment, your colleague is just as much your friend as they are your most duplicitous enemy. To get to the top of the career ladder, serpents divorce themselves from human emotions that can expose them to weakness. In fact, the majority of their frailties and shortcomings can be traced back to earthly corporeal feelings inherent in mankind, but their transmogrification into a serpent quells their compassion and moral integrity and compels them to pursue unrivalled prestige and an abundance of wealth.

Academic settings are fertile breeding grounds for next-generation serpents. The ambition to outshine their peers through high grades and entrepreneurial initiative can be evident as young as the early teens. When hatchlings are fully grown they never stay still for long because they always have places to go and people to see. They'll rush down Tube escalators, force their way onto trains regardless of limited space, and destroy colleagues with false kindness and Machiavellian deception. They care little for allowing the elderly access to a priority seat, as the holy grail for any serpent is to answer to no one and to be feared by everyone.

Why is this all relevant, you ask? Because YouTube stardom and the success that comes with it are simply too difficult for serpents to address. Belittling it or acting as if this career path isn't worthy of trying to fathom are the classic signs of cold-blooded jealousy. Serpents come in all shapes and sizes – they can be colleagues, friends, or even family – and one thing I've learned from having a life online is how to deal with people who look down on it. I'm well aware that my tone over the last few paragraphs has been enormously pissy, but I think it's important to be honest about the hardships of being a YouTuber. I've noticed that so many of us have ditched the term 'YouTuber' altogether and replaced it with 'influencer'. I'm personally not a fan. It makes me sound like I lure children into sewers dressed as a clown. But the preconceived negative connotations of 'YouTuber', and the unwanted attention it brings at US Customs, have in the past forced me to adapt my job title. Here's a quick list of occupations I've used:

Offline editor
Social Media Strategist
Data Communications Consultant
Search Engine Optimisation Analyst
Digital Marketing Specialist
Astronaut
Icon

The amount of time I've spent trying to enter America explaining how I make money from YouTube has seriously encroached on my holiday time. Is that not the most unforgivable First World problem you've ever heard?

Like in any job, underperform and you're out. YouTube is a public popularity contest, and I can completely understand why so many influencers feel obligated to make content that's not a true reflection of themselves but seems a safe option to stay above water. But before I criticise them from atop Pedro, my highest of horses, I'm aware that we've all been guilty of posting clickbait, though some more often than others. For the repeat offenders, I speak for everyone when I say, 'Fool me once, shame on you. Fool me twice, shame on you . . . only more.' I'm well aware that's not how the saying goes, but I refuse to accept blame for taking the bait when these titles are so deliciously deceptive. I for one am guilty for clicking on something I know full well is cheap chicanery, but I relish pinpointing the moment when the clickbait becomes clear, and I'm one to savour something that fuels my rage.

My own anger management issues aside, the success of false advertising can be incredibly difficult to compete with as a creator, regardless of the way it is bound to limit your shelf life. The only weapons at your disposable are your thumbnail and title: the popularity of a video relies purely on the way it's marketed, and as much as it saddens me, sex usually sells above all else.

I've come to realise that honest content is key. I'd much prefer a video that underperformed because boobs weren't in the thumbnail than feeling like I'd deceived my audience into watching bland, mediocre content. This deception had a far greater presence within the community than even I had imagined. It seemed that YouTubers were deceiving their viewers so lavishly and so often, that even other creators didn't know what was staged and what wasn't. This really hit home for me one summer when I was in Los Angeles and Grace Helbig, comedienne extraordinaire, striped T-shirt enthusiast and part-time model, spoke of how she'd not been entirely sure if my and Rosie's relationship was real until we'd met in person and she'd realised our chemistry couldn't be faked. I had no idea that people staged relationships because it was a formula that brought so much online attention and financial reward, yet when I was in Los Angeles it seemed that this was plausible, if not expected.

YouTube was becoming a business, and people were starting to create their own business models. I absolutely hated this. Straight girls were starting to queerbait, and real couples on the verge of breaking up were falsifying relationship bliss. 'Fake it until you make it' had never seemed so fitting. As a result, my cynicism was through the roof, and I'd become someone who had no faith in other people. How needlessly melodramatic. I do, however, stand by it, as my cynicism was later vindicated when our good natures were abused.

I believe in life we should never be judged by what we look like, only by the things we say and the way we act. If you have the choice to treat people well, why wouldn't you? It's free! It might be difficult when someone's reputation precedes them, but my motto is 'Tolerable until twat', a less sophisticated version of 'Innocent until proven guilty.' But it was our trusting nature and the way we wanted to believe in others that led to getting screwed on so many occasions, when colleagues turned into friends, friends turned back into colleagues, who then turned into opportunistic monsters. Not mixing business with friendship was a tough lesson we had to learn the hard way.

But we've also mixed business with our relationship, which has worked out great! So with every cloud there's a silver lining! You'd think, as with 'curry pasta', Rosie's brand of fusion cooking, it would be a recipe for disaster. But who would have thought that the combination of my seventeen-year-old self's passion for honest, intrusive filmmaking and a lesbian relationship would provide me with such an unexpected and exhilarating career path! Let's hope it doesn't provide me with a bunion . . . Although that in turn would provide me with a poetic sequel to one of my finest pieces of work.

ROSIE

YouTube wasn't something I planned to do as a full-time job because I never considered it a tangible career option. Not that I had many. At school, during Careers Week, we got to input all of our strengths and achievements into a computer program, which was supposed to spit out a list of job possibilities that were suitable for our personal abilities. My number-one career suggestion? Window cleaner.

Ever since I was little I've been a performer. My defining moment was in my primary-school Christmas nativity, when I played Angel Number Three. I delivered my one and only line, 'But we've GOT to think of SOMETHING!', in an American accent and received the largest roar of laughter from the crowd. I was famous.

I believed I was destined to be an actress. My mum insisted I do my A levels, instead of attending drama school, so that I'd have a safety net. She reminded me how tough the competition was when it came to acting. That everyone had what I had, and possibly more. I could act and dance, but some people could act, dance and sing. Worse still, some people could act, dance and sing to a much better standard than I could. I didn't give up my dream, but in the meantime, I decided to work hard. I also got a real job.

One of my first jobs was working as a cleaner at my own school. It seemed the computer program wasn't that inaccurate after all. I was in sixth form at the time, and it meant I'd get up and go to school from 9 a.m. until 3.30 p.m., at which point I would watch forlornly as everyone left, while I opened the cleaning cupboard and dragged out the Hoover. I would clean up my own classmates' mess until 6 p.m. every day, and it was embarrassing to say the least. I can distinctly remember the day I refused to clean off something that was stuck to the wall of the science-block boys' toilets. I remember it well, not just because Caretaker Graham laughed and claimed it was 'just spit', but because it was juxtaposed with seeing one of my classmates driving off in his brand-new Audi with a personalised number plate. I grew up with little, and I learned the meaning of hard work early on.

My next job was as a cashier at a German supermarket well known for hurling people's shopping items past the scanner as quickly as possible. I'm not going to lie, probably all of my self-hatred and bad times in life stem from working at Lidl. I'll never forget the time I was sitting at the till when my ex-boyfriend – we'll call him Shmike – walked up to me and said, 'Living the dream I see, Spaughton.' How dare he? Well, Shmike, look at me now. I have a blue tick by my name on Twitter AND Instagram, so I think that makes a pretty strong twenty-first-century statement. I'm just kidding, those things don't mean anything. But Shmike, you're still a dick.

I worked some rubbish jobs for a while but I wanted much more for myself. After sixth form I went to university to get my degree in Media and Cultural Studies. Just before enrolling in my second year of university, I started dating Rose, which changed the course of my life for ever. It was a whirlwind, and together we tumbled down the rabbit hole and landed in a world of romance and silliness, where we documented every high and every low of our relationship online. We fell in love, and caught every moment on camera.

YouTube was Rose's thing before I came along, as her college had set her a project to make a viral video. She had a camera, a skill set comprising zoom-ins and editing, and most importantly, she had passion. She was good at what she did and she knew it, and I found that irresistible.

Rose used making videos as an excuse to date me. She'd say, 'I have to see you next Friday because we have to film another video,' and that's how our YouTubing began. We'd sit down in front of the camera, forget the camera was there, flirt outrageously and have a great time. Then Rose would upload the videos and people would comment on them. It was a weird feeling to think that strangers from around the world were taking an interest in our coversations. Why were they watching? It was surreal to receive such positive reactions to what I thought of as just two girls hanging out and oversharing beyond the bounds of acceptability!

After months of uploading videos we discovered it was possible to earn money from YouTube. It was never our driving force, it's not why we began, and it never affected the nature of our content. We remained outspoken, dangerously honest and not safe for work! Earning money was merely an added bonus of doing something we loved! Our first payment was £20, which, naturally, we split down the middle: we went to Iceland and spent it on chicken biryani, wine gums and alcohol. When we hit 200,000 subscribers – and I honestly don't know how that happened – we got signed to an MCN, which stands for 'multi-channel network' and is an organisation that takes a percentage of your earnings in exchange for helping you grow your audience. Back then, lots of YouTubers were getting ripped off, as they'd sign away up to 50 per cent of their earnings in long-term contracts and get no extra exposure in return. We were amongst those YouTubers. Our MCN did encourage us to upload regularly . . . and that's about all they had to offer. So, we started trying to upload every week. Eventually, we'd earned enough money to afford a better camera, sharper lighting and a decent microphone. It's great to look professional, but seeing as some of our best content is caught off guard, I wasn't too bothered about all that. But with that being said, we still wanted to deliver the best content we could, and being in focus certainly wasn't going to hurt!

We continued to upload as often as we could for the next two years, never paying much attention to popular trends or video challenges, but continuing to do what we enjoyed: chatting amongst ourselves about everything and nothing. We still didn't really understand how the platform worked but were confident that people wanted to see us talk openly about our lives. The moment I would say we actually became 'YouTubers' was when we started doing it full-time. Rose made the leap first, which was only fair, because back then she did all the editing and did more work in general. She was working her first full-time job after graduating at a premium Apple retailer, and would spend her two days off filming and editing. It got to the point where she had no free time. We'd also just launched our merchandise shop, at the request of our subscribers, and did absolutely *everything* ourselves, which included sourcing the clothing, designing the print, running the online shop and posting all the orders! Our house was full of printing labels and clothes were stacked everywhere. Don't even get me started on our trips to the post office. We practically lived there.

There was no way we could continue to spread our time and energy between working full-time, then coming home and working full-time again on our YouTube career. Rose went away on holiday with her sister, and I guess the time out made her realise how difficult it would be to come back home and go back to juggling it all. YouTube was nearly bringing in as much money as Rose's job, and although she wanted to take the plunge, she was nervous. But when it came down to it, YouTube was her passion. We both enjoyed creating content so much more than our other jobs, and that's what pushed her to quit. You don't get anywhere if you don't try!

Rose left her job in April 2014 but I didn't quit mine until March the following year. I had my first 'proper' career job, doing social media for a top UK marketing company, and I really enjoyed working in a professional setting, in a sector related to my degree. It allowed me the opportunity to be creative and to learn even more about the technical aspects of search engine optimisation! I booked time off for our wedding, and after that for our honeymoon, but I never returned. Around the same time, we were auditioning to become presenters of *The Xtra Factor* (we made it down to the last five, and I'm proud of that to this day!) and were also considering moving to London, as we were regularly making the three-hour train journey for meetings with our new management. We didn't know if we could afford to live in London, or if this would all work out as a career, but we didn't want to miss out on the opportunity. We decided we would move closer to the city, give it a year, and if we couldn't afford it we would move back home. Well, so far so good! Sometimes you have to 'Be bold and mighty forces will come to your aid.' I stole that quote from *Pretty Little Liars*. (Google also tells me it's by someone called Basil King.)

Every day is different, which is fantastic because my Gemini spirit gets bored easily. Some days we'll wake up, decide to stay in our pyjamas, and edit in bed with copious cups of tea, or other days we'll get up early and spend the day in London, having meetings, and getting excited about future projects. But just chatting in front of the camera is still one of my favourite things to do. Sometimes we work with brands, which we really enjoy because it challenges us. Obviously brands want us to sell their product to our audience, so let me say first of all that we'd never advertise anything that we personally dislike or think that any one else will. For a sponsored video we have to find creative ways to make it entertaining and funny, yet hit all the criteria that we've agreed upon. I honestly love it. When our viewers leave comments saying it was a great video, and the brand tells me they were all laughing at it in the office, it makes me glow with pride. In a world where not every brand or company champions diversity, I'm happy to work with most brands who see our primarily LGBT audience as a priority, rather than a minority not worth selling to.

We often attend conventions like VidCon or Summer in the City, where we're invited to speak on panels. YouTube has brought us opportunities that have truly tested our nerves! I can remember the first time we spoke publicly, in 2014 at Summer in the City, and I nearly fainted under the pressure! I could feel sweat rolling down the back of my neck, and I remember fearing that when it was my turn to speak no words would come out. Now I feel confident that I am able to sit on panels and discuss serious issues, in the hope of making a difference – topics such as female empowerment, coming out, and how to deal with homophobia and cyberbullying.

Now Rose and I even have our own live stage show that we have taken on tour. YouTube truly has pushed us and helped us to grow. Don't get me wrong, we still suffer from nerves, and I have to take it out on the toilet before we go onstage *every time*. But I'm constantly learning. My biggest fears are: falling over on stage, soiling myself on stage, or, and this one is my worst nightmare, accidentally offending/upsetting people. Rose and I discuss very sensitive issues, and the last thing I would want to do is make anyone go away feeling unhappy. The responsibility is huge, and we should never take lightly the power of our words.

Lately this has been at the forefront of my mind. As our audience has expanded, so has my conscience, which has been both a good thing and a bad thing. On the one hand, it's wonderful to be self-aware; to consider others' feelings and how they might react to something I say or do online. However, if I'm honest, it can also be scary. I've seen other YouTubers have old tweets or things they've said in the past dragged up, splashed across newspaper headlines or retweeted on Twitter. I'm going to be straight up with you right now: I am not a perfect person. I have most definitely said or done things in the past that I regret. Small things that most people do get magnified when you are in the spotlight. The internet loves a good witch hunt. If someone in the public eye has ever said something stupid, rude or mean, it can get blown out of proportion. But not everything is black and white, and no one has lived their life completely devoid of any flaw or mistake.

Looking back at myself online, I can literally see myself growing up. I try to avoid watching back old videos because they are cringey. It's weird having a video record of yourself – weekly videos over a number of years. I see my style changing, my make-up application getting better, my points of view changing. I also see my relationship with Rose evolving, and I think that's what others see too. That's something so precious and wonderful that YouTube has given me. I hope that when I'm old and grey-haired with nothing to do, I can just sit there and watch the good times again.

But let's talk some more about the one thing that people always want to ask YouTubers about. Money. Spoiler: being a YouTuber is a job; we all earn different amounts. We're all working at different levels, have different knowledge about the platform, and we all work our way up at different paces.

I hate the money question more than I hate those people who try to tell you that you'd probably recovered from the cold you've been suffering with for weeks but then reinfected yourself with the same cold. 'You probably got over it but then reinfected your-self.' NO. THAT'S NOT HOW COLDS WORK, JAN.

In any other profession, asking how much someone earns is usually regarded as socially unacceptable, and yet the rules seem to change when it comes to YouTube. I find it bizarre how people seem to consider it their right to know, and I'm unsure why there's an element of shaming surrounding how much we earn from the content we make, usually following a brutal interrogation.

The most disheartening thing for me is the assumption that YouTubers don't deserve the money they make, or the perks of their job. You have to remember that YouTube is a free platform, which means that Rose and I get up every day and put all our energy into creating videos that people can access at the click of a button. We don't charge people for our content, so it's nice that our audience can watch for free and we still get paid for our creativity. YouTube is the job of a lifetime, but just because it's incredibly rewarding doesn't mean it's easy.

Another thing that upsets me is the general assumption that YouTubers are 'lazy' and that all we do is create a 'five-minute video' once a week. This especially hurts because it negates all the talent and dedication that goes into sustaining a YouTube channel. Sure, YouTube is a free platform, which means that technically anybody can become a YouTuber. But to be able to create videos that appeal to a mass audience and then to sustain that audience takes hard work. Rose and I have three channels, and it typically takes around an hour to film a video, and sometimes days or weeks of filming for a vlog. Editing usually takes two days minimum, and like most people in their jobs, we have deadlines to work to. And once your videos are live, you have to continue to create and upload entertaining videos. Rose and I are in a constant battle against ourselves, to 'out-do' each video we upload. We strive to make them funnier, snappier, sillier. *We are* the process from start to finish. We conceptualise, we shoot, we light, we direct, we edit, we upload. Some people even act as their own manager, responding to emails and negotiating with companies and brands.

Of all my jobs, I have never experienced pressure like I have with YouTube. Recently, on a trip back home, I saw my grandad, and he did the typical, extremely condescending grown-up thing of saying to me, 'Stressed? You? You're young, you have nothing to be stressed about!'

At the time of writing this, I'm ill. Not just feeling-a-bit-under-the-weather poorly, but Rose is sleeping in another bedroom, life is a constant stream of throbbing headaches and sweaty night-mares, my phlegm is luminous green, and my throat is raw. 'So what?' you might say. 'Everyone gets poorly.' True, but we're about to go on tour and people have bought tickets! Not only that, but some people have bought flights and booked hotels. I can't let them down, and that's high-pressure stuff! I have back-to-back shows to perform and a two-hour meet and greet before each one, and I need my voice, even if it's often several decibels higher than it should be. My succession of migraines isn't helping, and there's not a lot you can get done when you're blind and bedridden!

But the idea of failing to deliver what our audience has invested their time and money into isn't an option for me. The support they've shown us and the encouragement they offer makes the harder times a lot less difficult.

An excellent example of the kinds of high-stress situations Rose and I have dealt with is when we were about to interview Melissa McCarthy and Paul Feig about their upcoming film *Ghostbusters*. We had been planning it for months, going over and over our questions on our dog walks. We'd put so much effort into thinking up creative questions that would sell the film but would also be interesting to our audience. Five minutes before we went into the interview we were told we weren't able to ask any of our pre-planned questions and that we'd have to start completely from scratch. I can remember the cold sweat prickling on the back of my neck as Rose and I started wracking our brains for ideas, realising we had no time to learn new questions by heart. Fortunately we managed not to crumble, and I think we totally smashed it!

But I'm not complaining. Alongside the enormous pressure, YouTube brings extreme highs. But nothing, and I mean NOTHING, beats the rush of meeting our audience. Of hearing a crowd cheer, of seeing faces laughing, or listening, ready for the next surprise. Our first UK tour was the most intense, exhilarating, nerve-wracking, surprising and heartwarming thing we've ever done. Coming back to our empty house after ten days of being completely engrossed in our audience was like waking up with a shocking hangover and being slammed into a brick wall. After the pure highs of performing night after night, being constantly surrounded by a crowd of people, that adrenaline rush, coming back home was a shock to the system to say the least. Our job isn't 'normal' and it certainly isn't boring!

Being entertaining every day can be tough. Especially around Christmas, when vlogging every day has become a trend. A lot goes into it that you might not initially consider. Filming content isn't always a breeze. You don't always turn on the camera and instantly get movie magic. Sometimes when I edit my own face, I'm horrified by what I see. Editing yourself can be cringey, and you don't always want to watch something back, while other times you'll find you've captured nothing but gold! Rose and I have magical moments on camera, like the day we brought home our dog, Wilma, and the day Rose proposed to me. It's hard work, it's not as easy as it looks, but it is so incredible, having those special moments captured for ever.

Rose and I have a wonderful audience. I would even go so far as to say that our audience is better than anyone else's. Our demographic is 95 per cent female and our core audience ranges between fifteen and thirty-four years old, and they usually fall under the LGBTQ+ umbrella, though we obviously have viewers who are younger, older, male or straight, and we're certainly not exclusive! We strive to create content for everyone to enjoy!

I feel like our viewers are our support system. When we meet our audience they tell us stories of how watching us being a couple on YouTube has given them the courage to come out. People tell us that they've met their girlfriends or partners through watching our videos or coming to our shows, and I find that so incredible. But I feel that our audience give us just as much as we give them in return. They tell us our videos cheer them up, but it's their support that keeps us going. We'd never be in this position without them, and their tweets, messages, comments, videos and faces make me happy. It really is a two-way street.

Having such a wonderful audience makes us feel incredibly lucky and I suppose that's why any online hate or negative feed-back can come as quite a shock. Similar to the shock I felt when Camila said she was leaving Fifth Harmony. Rose and I get the occasional bit of nastiness in the comment section, sure. Some people are quite blunt and will simply say something no one would ever really say to someone's face without feeling awkward. 'You've put a lot of weight on,' for example, or my personal favourite, 'Shut it, I'll cum on your head.'

I don't really take these things to heart and I manage to brush them off quite easily. Negative comments about our content can be frustrating, especially when the odd few accuse us of 'selling out' or doing 'sooooo many ads' when in reality the non-branded content far outweighs our sponsored videos. But the hardest and most demoralising thing for me, and I imagine for Rose, was when we discovered a chat forum about ourselves in 2013. I was googling myself (which, I hasten to add, was nothing to do with vanity – I believe I was trying to see if my blog page came up when you searched my name) and I stumbled upon it. This chat forum was dedicated to LGBT YouTubers, and it is honestly something I wish I could stop my past self from discovering. Kate Moennig, whom you may know as Shane from *The L Word*, called this forum 'a place of cruelty' and she wasn't wrong. This forum, consisting of about seventeen to forty-five active users, tore us apart. They commented on everything I couldn't help about myself, and more. I read about how ugly and fat I was, then later got called 'anorexic'. They discussed how I wore too much make-up and that my hair was blonde and cheap-looking. I can admit that when it came to the latter, they had a point. I just wish they'd mentioned my eyebrows a little sooner so I could have saved me from myself. They were adamant that, as a bisexual, I was destined to leave Rose for a man. From watching a few of our videos, these people thought they knew everything about our lives, and how they could live them better than we were.

It was hard to tear ourselves away, even though it was so gut-wrenchingly awful. But imagine if you stumbled across a forum of anonymous people talking about you, discussing every little detail of your life and giving their feedback – wouldn't you be tempted to read it? It was like morbid fascination, and no matter how unhappy it made me, I couldn't allow my eyes to stop reading. One of the most difficult things about the forum was reading lies about myself. People would fabricate stories and spread them as preposterous rumours, and we were utterly defenceless as they tarnished our name. They made up false scenarios, like how they'd met Rose in London and she'd refused to take a photo with them. The hardest thing to read was about when Rose and I were supposed to attend a meet-and-greet event and Rose collapsed due to wrongly prescribed medicine. She was taking beta blockers to help her deal with nerves and to prevent panic attacks. But Rose has low blood pressure and the medicine was far too strong, and she ended up collapsing, being severely dehydrated and unable to attend. For weeks after, the forum discussed how 'disgusting' Rose was for 'partying so hard and getting drunk the night before the big event'. They called her an 'alcoholic' and said she didn't care about her fans who had paid money for tickets and travelled to the location. I honestly believe that the people who write on that forum are living extremely lonely lives. How sad it must be to be so bitter.

But onwards and upwards, and Rose and I banned the forum from our lives. The lesson learned, I suppose, is that by putting your life online you have to expect people to talk about you. They have a right to their own opinions, and people make assumptions. But those who spend their lives talking about the lives of others make me assume they might not have much of a life of their own, which in many ways I can sympathise with. The forum taught me how strong I am, and that you can't please everyone. All I can be is myself, and Rose and I are a lot happier now that we don't pay attention to it. We create the content we want to create, wear the clothes we want to wear, and are unashamedly ourselves, which is exactly how we started and how we mean to go on!

YouTube is a magical job which has offered us huge opportunities and has opened so many doors for us. One of my biggest dreams was to write a book, and here I am! I have YouTube to thank for that. Having an audience can get you noticed, and I've seen YouTubers become actors, directors, presenters, all off the back of their hard work building up their brand and their audience. However, lots choose to simply remain on the platform and are doing extremely well from it!

But the biggest thing that YouTube has brought into my life is the fact that I now run a business. I've learned that there's no point making plans in life, because life always has other plans for you. I never imagined I'd run a business, let alone with my own wife, but here we are. We originally only started the business because we had just opened our online merchandise store and didn't know how to pay tax on the extra money we were earning. A family friend suggested we get an accountant, and let them create a business for us and handle all of the scary adult stuff, so that's exactly what we did.

It's strange having a business that's essentially your relationship and the documentation of your real life. It can be really difficult seeing that as your 'brand'. It feels almost uncomfortable calling it that without running the risk of our content sounding inauthentic or calculated. What I can say is that we *always* have our viewers' interests at heart. Rose and I want to create content that people will enjoy, and that we enjoy creating. If we can help people in the process, provide comfort or alleviate life's burdens just for a moment, that's even better. It's been a learning curve, and we've definitely made some wrong decisions along the way. We've trusted the wrong people, and had people use us for fame or money, and that's been upsetting. But we've grown wiser, and have learned how to ask the right questions. We've got sharper, we pay closer attention, and we constantly consider the outcome. I think I originally felt slightly ashamed to stand up for myself – I felt so lucky to be doing what I was doing that I didn't want to push it. But now I dream big, I make goals and I attempt to smash them! This year has been the most exciting year of our YouTube career so far. It's been the busiest, we've worked on the most exciting projects, and you know things are going well when you have to cancel two holidays because you have so much work to do! I've been tired, stressed and ill, but I wouldn't change a thing because I KNOW that Rose and I are creating things that will make a difference. I'm absolutely in love with YouTube – and being able to do it all alongside the love of my life? Well, Shmike, I really am living the dream.

CHAPTER 4
MENTAL HEALTH

'When life seems gloomy, turn up the brightness.'
(It's F2 on a Mac.)

ROSE

The brain. An organ so smart it named itself. It has the power to play tricks on us, to inhibit, to exaggerate, to control and to make us believe sagging pants and shutter shades were high fashion. We know relatively little about the human brain. What we do know is that our mental health has a profound effect on our stability, our happiness, our potential and our relationships. In this chapter, Rosie and I will be sharing our most personal experiences, things we've never discussed online. I hope some of this will resonate with you, and will encourage you to believe that we needn't be held back by our thoughts or conditions. We can be the master of them.

I'm a strong believer that everything happens for a reason. Why did I grow a tiny goat beard when I was nineteen? Hormone imbalance. But I'm also a firm believer that you can't always know the reason for something while you're going through it. When I was sixteen I faced the darkest time of my life. This was way beyond discovering I was gay or losing Mufasa to crazed wildebeest. It was beyond any anxiety I had previously felt, and I thought it would result in the end of my life. After working so hard for my glowing

GSCE results, something triggered my brain to implode and canni-
balise itself in the summer of 2004. Because my head was no longer
full of GSCE revision, my mind unexpectedly went into overdrive
and filled with thoughts I seemingly had no control over. Violent,
upsetting, intrusive thoughts that made me question my entire
being and moral code. On the surface I appeared normal. On the
inside I was spiralling out of control.

Why was this happening? What did it mean? My mind was full
of unwanted images, scenarios and outcomes that terrified me so
much I lost total grip on reality. I suffered from 'episodes' when I'd
fall so far into fear-induced spiralling that I'd get stuck there for
hours. I'd have an unwanted thought then I'd analyse what it meant,
why it was there and how it could manifest into reality. I assumed
that the thoughts I had were a forewarning because I was going
to act on them. After months of such debilitating distress, I had a
mental breakdown so severe I tried to take my own life. Twice.

As my brain became riddled with darkness, my conscience had
all of a sudden kicked into overdrive, and I obsessively began to
ruminate over every potentially dark thought or image I'd ever had
in my mind throughout my lifetime. I tried to find links from my
childhood to suggest that the sudden influx of unwanted thoughts
was because I was a bad person. This idea of being morally deplor-
able haunted me, and grew into something I was totally unable to
manage. What was happening?! I was terrified of myself. I couldn't
be in any social setting because I felt too guilty to converse with
other people. I slept all day, and ate through my crippling anxiety.
My mind was in turmoil, nothing made sense, and my life as I knew
it was over. I grieved for a time when guilt hadn't consumed my life.
I wasn't living any more. I was simply existing, haunted by feelings of
disgrace.

The only way I could cope with one of my regular day-to-day
panic attacks was to press my fingernails into the skin on my arm,
but by the time it was over, the damage I'd left was far worse than
just indent marks. Forgive the graphic nature of this sentence, but I

would scratch away up to seven layers of skin just to feel a different sensation than panic. It was something physical I could focus on. This self-harm escalated, and I was forced to wear sweat bands around my wrists if ever we had company. I never cut, I scratched. These wounds resembled burns. They wept, but I enjoyed the constant reminder that I was being punished. It was less work for my mind.

After suffering in silence, I spoke to Laura about what I was going through. She reassured me by telling me about a mental health disability called obsessive compulsive disorder. It didn't come as much of a comfort. I was so deep into this disorder that I couldn't see outside of it, or how I could blame it for my thoughts. Something was happening to me and I was spiralling out of control. I was so worried I was going to hurt someone, or break the law, or have to accept something about myself that was far worse than being gay. Accepting that I was dangerous wasn't an option for me. If that was where this was leading, I knew I had to end my life.

Weight piled on, the darkness in my mind remained, and my struggle continued for years. Mum and Dad were aware of the situation and accepted that they would live their lives caring for me as if I were both mentally and physically disabled. Physically, because I didn't move. I had no confidence because I'd gained so much weight. I had no space in my mind for anything other than my intrusive thoughts and the rumination that followed. As a result I sacrificed my higher learning, dropped out of sixth form and spent two years at home within the safety of my bedroom's four walls. It took that long for me to feel that I could leave the house alone. My whole life suffered and my world had shrunk.

During that period Laura came with me to see a doctor. I've never heard of a doctor referring a patient to a psychologist so quickly. I met some extremely entertaining individuals throughout my two years of therapy. One was the 'recent graduate' brand of psychotherapist, who helped me greatly by responding to my traumatising thought confessions with 'Hmmmm . . .' As I waited for her to respond with something constructive to alleviate my guilt and anxiety, I'd be forced to fill the silence with a potential answer to my own question, to which she'd then respond, 'Hmmmm . . .' We'd go full circle: I'd voice a worry, come up with a uneducated answer, run it by her to see if that correlated with any of the texts she'd read in her years of studying the brain, and she'd round everything off with an inconclusive 'Hmmmm . . .' Excellent. Absolutely worth the months I'd spent on the waiting list.

I've had very different experiences of therapy, so I shan't bash it excessively. Some of my most positive experiences followed the darkest days I've ever faced.

When I think about the following story now, it's actually hilarious, but at the time it was a truly heartbreaking moment for me. Life had become so unbearable that I decided to end it. I rummaged through the medicine cabinet and found a jar of pills I assumed were painkillers. I cried, not because I wanted to die, but because I wanted to live. I swallowed twenty-three tablets, which I assumed were enough to do the job, and lay down on my sister's bed and waited. When my dad came home from work he came upstairs and calmly asked me what was wrong. I started to panic. I told him what I'd done and he started to cry. Soon Mum was on the case, and when Barbara Denise Dix needs to sort something out, not even dragon's breath or the hammer of an ill-tempered troll could deter her. In fact, she seemed to embody both as she transformed into a tidal wave of practicality and focus, with a pinch of impatient telephone manner. Lots of things were running through my head: I'd never know how *Lost* ended, I'd never pursue magic, but, most importantly, what had I actually taken?

All became clear when my mum picked up the empty pill bottle in a frenzy. She immediately rang the hospital, who told her not to worry. Of course I needed help in a mental capacity – I'd just tried to kill myself . . . which indicated that I wasn't happy. But physically I was going to be just fine. As if the mental exhaustion of OCD, the physical exertion of chronic depression and my brand-new stretch marks weren't enough, but now I'd gone and swallowed twenty-three discoloured vitamin D tablets, which were about to give me three weeks of constipation and the possibility of an anal fissure. Marvellous! If life wasn't shit enough, now I couldn't even poo properly and enjoy that.

Shortly afterwards I saw my therapist, who seemed concerned by my failed attempt. I knew she was perturbed by my behaviour from the 'Hmmmm ...' she exhaled, in what seemed to be an actual thought process and not just the easy way out of offering something constructive. She prescribed me diazepam. Problem solved! But I decided not to take it, as I was still full from my vitamin D amuse-bouche and didn't it turn out to be amusing!

I was obviously really rubbish at committing suicide, so my next attempt took a slightly more poetic approach. I didn't want to have to experience the inconvenience of pain, constipation or a Sylvia Plath-style oven embrace, so I thought it best to rely on the elements. I thought nothing could be easier than stepping outside in my pyjamas and waiting for the frost nip to do the job those two-faced vitamins had failed to do. I was very serious. I left the house in my pyjamas and slippers (not dissimilar to Rosie's late-night dog-walking ensemble), and headed towards the river. I didn't want to jump in: that was far too dramatic, and possibly life-threatening. No, I'd wait. I would wait until I froze to death in a sophisticated, uptown manner. There were a number of problems I didn't think I'd face with this foolproof plan. Number one: how long was this going to take? And number two: I was starting to get cold. If there was a way this could have worked out slightly closer to room temperature, that would have been great.

I began second-guessing my stratagem. Being this cold was unpleasant. It also occurred to me that I'd left the house without telling my parents that I was off to kill myself and not to wait up. They were probably starting to get worried. I gave it a solid forty minutes. I told myself that if it took any longer than an hour then this method was far too time-consuming, and I'd re-evaluate my options at a later date. Freezing to death wasn't as easy as I thought it would be. I was really cold, which was unexpected. I was also really bored and hadn't thought to bring any in-flight entertainment, which was obviously a failure in judgement. The cold was beginning to hurt my toes, and the last thing I wanted to do was make life harder for myself by losing a few and having to develop a pirate's walk. I decided the best course of action was to return home. That multipack of Mars Bars wasn't going to eat itself – I couldn't forget my commitments. I also had a commitment to my parents, but when you're depressed you become selfish, and other people's feelings aren't your first priority. Chocolate, however, is. I had somewhere to be.

As I walked through the door, my mother broke down in tears. I'll never forget what she said to me. 'I think you're having a break-down, Sausage.' Not a great time to comment on my weight. I kid, Sausage has always been her pet name for me. Quite ironic really, considering my preference. Jokes aside, she was right. I was certainly having a breakdown. How could I have left a multipack. We hugged it out and talked it through, and together we agreed that a different therapist was in order. I'll also never forget the words Mum said to me further down the line: 'You're just going to have to buck up and try harder to get over it.' This was exactly what I needed to hear. Yes, it was going to be difficult, but I wasn't having much luck wallowing in my own self-pity and the smell of wet dog, which was fast becoming my personal aroma.

Don't get my mother wrong, she was extremely patient and sympathetic with my issues. She had all the time in the world for me and went to great lengths to make sure I was all right. If there was a problem, she wanted to solve it. But at this stage, her panic had set in and she tried a slightly different tack. During these dark days the bond we had was very strong. Countless times we'd cuddle on her bed when I was in the midst of an anxiety attack or a big cry. She'd help me treat the wounds I'd inflicted on my arms and try to dissuade me from doing it again. Laura was also a fantastic help. While she was saving for her master's degree (in Excessive

Higher Learning), she worked at the local doctor's surgery for a year. I called her so many times a day that I knew her work number by heart. She was brilliant at taking away the panic which followed an unwanted thought, but I was relying on her far too much. Not once did she ever lose her patience with me, but it was time for me to see a different psychologist, one who specialised in psychology because I'd heard that could help.

In came Estelle, who was brilliant. She explained what OCD was, how it worked, why it manifested, how my brain was different, and ways to conquer it. She was extremely bright. I trusted she'd be able to help because she seemed knowledgable and eager to know more about me. On our second meeting I presented her with a 3,000-word essay detailing everything I'd ever thought, felt or done, however minor, for which I wanted forgiveness. It took me two weeks to pluck up the courage to list these things and revisit them, and when I handed her my perfectly worded thesis, it felt like a weight had been lifted.

So why wasn't she prising it from my frostnip-recovering finger-tips and treating it like the best goss a patient could ever give their therapist? I was basically handing her my life on a plate, and all I wanted in return was a professional to tell me that I was a perfect person with a totally clean moral slate. Frustratingly, she didn't even give it a pity glance. I mean, I was a busy woman too, but in between watching *Finding Nemo* on repeat and drinking saturated fat, I'd still managed to find the time to document my existence for her benefit. I told her how hard it had been to write, how guilty I felt for my thoughts, and that it would benefit me greatly if she could just take a look.

She told me it wouldn't benefit me at all. It was my turn to say, 'Hmmmm . . .' She told me that her justifying my thoughts, feelings and actions would incentivise me to 'confess' every 'sin' I ever thought I'd committed to every single person I met throughout my lifetime. If anything, the short-term alleviation of guilt would actually make the idea of 'confession' more powerful, and in my broken mind it might become a social necessity, and that was the exact behaviour she would never encourage. Smart lady. She made me rip it up in front of her. It was the most powerful moment I'd had in my entire life. More powerful than the *Homeward Bound* Sassy survival reveal. I didn't need forgiveness, I needed to realise I had nothing that *needed* forgiving. Difficult to appreciate when your head is full of dreadful thoughts and fears, but it paved the way for a new way of thinking.

I soon began to feel comfortable with having OCD. Comfortable with knowing I had a condition that made me highly analytical, a total perfectionist, and overall a good person. My therapist told me that the majority of OCD sufferers worry about thinking or doing the sorts of things they're least likely to do. For example, new mothers worry they'll purposefully harm their child. But actually these mothers are the furthest from ever acting on such a thought or fear. The fear itself is so great, and is so far from the reality they'd wish for, that their mind is overwhelmed and plagued by fear and rumination.

As I was beginning to understand my condition in greater detail, I decided to embark on a course of group therapy, just for LOLs, and there I met characters I'll never forget. It was like a sitcom about a coffee morning at an asylum, and I say that with respect. I shan't use anyone's real names, because most of them came from the Forest of Dean and I wouldn't be able to spell them anyway, so let's fabricate a few. We had Nigel, who was obsessed with the sound of running taps after a particularly aggressive house flooding; Sarah, who couldn't touch any products from Morrisons, convinced that it would result in the loss of her children in a custody battle; and Samantha, who feared toys in the middle of the carpet. I respected all of them, but found them FASCINATING. If anything, the comedy gold I found in each of their individual stories made it easier to think that, to someone else, my concerns were equally as ridiculous. The links they were making were so nonsensical and nonexistent that it made me realise how irrational my own fears were. That's a little harder to prove when it's your own moral code up for debate, rather than the supernatural curse of a Morrisons Battenberg, but still. I deemed group therapy a success! My therapist wanted to test Nigel's progress by leaving the tap on just enough that it dripped but didn't run. But this made Nigel sweat excessively which in itself resulted in dripping, so it truly was a double blow for him. We never told Sarah the biscuits provided at our sessions came from Morrisons, because that probably would have been counterproductive. In hindsight, it would have made a fab YouTube prank.

It was impossible at the time to imagine that I was going through such a horrible, debilitating experience for any other reason than it was the hand life had dealt me. But I like to believe that it happened for a reason, and even though it was the scariest, lone-liest and darkest time of my life, I am actually grateful for it. Like being gay, OCD doesn't define me, but it certainly contributes to my personality. Luckily, I've managed to turn most of the traits that used to hinder me into positives that propel me closer to achiev-ing my dreams. For example, you won't find anyone who can tell something is parallel BY EYE better than RoseCD (a nickname I was given at college). Being a perfectionist used to completely disable me. Creating nothing was better than creating something that wasn't 'perfect'. Now I've managed to use that perfectionism, and not let it stifle me but let it inspire me to be the best that I can be. Doing my best regardless of the outcome is enough to feel satisfied with myself. I have extremely high standards when it comes to what I expect to achieve, but that has only benefited me as an adult. As the saying goes, 'Shoot for the moon. Even if you miss you'll land amongst the stars.' Unless it's actually the illusion of stars that have already burned out . . . that would be so unfortunate.

One of the best things I was ever told was that I'd have this condition for ever. Although the thought of that was terrifying, I was far too backed up to shit myself about it, so I made peace with having to adapt and move forward rather than sit still and resent my life! But moving forward, facing your fears and trying to make a success of yourself can be incredibly nerve-wracking stuff. This industry has really tested me. It's pushed me out of my comfort zone, which has resulted in tremendous rewards, pride and satisfaction, but still, with each venture there is a constant battle with anxiety.

I now try to follow my fear, rather than being restricted by it, because it usually leads to the best places! I'd never have ended up at the Yard House in Miami to end our North American tour if I'd let my fear of flying stand in my way. And then I'd never have experienced cheese curds with a bourbon-and-honey dipping sauce, and what's a life without that? (Apart from one with a lower risk of heart disease. Sounds boring.) As humans we tend to avoid the things that induce the most fear. Our fight-or-flight mechanism can often malfunction when we wrongly determine that a situation will cause us harm.

My fight-or-flight response is somewhat literal, in that my desire for 'flight' usually kicks in during a flight. How can I get away from the thing that's getting *me* away?! And there's nothing like travelling in a tin-can germ pool with no exits to make you feel safe. For me, it's a nightmare. I'm completely devoid of control. I have to put all my trust in another human being – how incomprehensible is that? We're forced to interact with the people around us because we're breathing their stale recycled air which is slowly growing into a protein culture. And the only thing that can break up a deep vein thrombosis and developing spores is the turbulence that impairs my central nervous system. I've had some truly harrowing aeroplane experiences. I envy Rosie, who can quite happily relax to the point of falling asleep with her mouth open before take-off. I don't know when I developed such a profound fear of flying, but then again, I don't know when I was first afraid of Alanis Morissette.

The way I cope with travelling abroad is to obsess over the

contents of my hand luggage. This, in addition to the clothes I wear, is the only thing I can control on a flight. I take great care to make sure my white trainers are truly white, and that every item of my outfit is freshly washed. If I'm going to die, I want to smell good doing it – and it may even improve my chances.

One of the hardest things I've had to harness is my relation-ship with superstition. OCD sufferers tend to make powerful links between our positive or negative experiences and events that have not contributed to their eventuality in the slightest. But we attribute these outcomes to events that have affected us so strongly that we tend to repeat behaviour to try and assure ourselves that we will be safe. It's like relying on a lucky charm for a good exam result, but on overdrive. For example, before our flight to Costa Rica I noticed I had a splash of cooking oil on the T-shirt I'd planned to wear on the plane, and spent the next hour assessing the situation so I could devise a plan. It wasn't as easy as choosing a different top to wear; I had to decide whether I wanted the unclean garment destroyed, hexed or banished to a hell dimension.

The frustrating part of my condition is knowing that my behaviour is irrational but that I'm not brave enough to break the cycle. I'm told that intelligence has no bearing on being able to achieve this, and that my brain simply can't send and receive rational cognitive messaging as easily as the average human. I assume this is because I'm way above average.

One of the most uncomfortable lessons I learned in group therapy was about stamping out superstitious reasoning. On the whiteboard in front of us, Estelle, my softly spoken psychiatrist, wrote that her husband would die that day in a car crash. She asked those of us who believed it was going to happen to raise our hands. I paused. With a passion for private investigation, first I glanced at her ring finger to make sure that she was in fact married. There was a ring. But nothing confirmed whether or not she was married to a man, so it remained inconclusive as to whether she was lying about her flippant ability to risk the life of her loved one.

My cynicism aside, the temptation to raise my hand was too great, and up it flew. Estelle turned to me and asked me to explain how these two things were rationally linked. Well, I had a pretty solid answer . . . 'They're linked because my parents taught me never to underestimate the power of your words.'

Estelle paused momentarily. Sarah's insides were screaming. Not because she cared about Estelle's 'husband', but because it wasn't clear whether the whiteboard came from Morrisons. Estelle said that it was very possible her husband would die that day, but if it were to happen, her having written it down would have no bearing on that unfortunate outcome. I giggled for a fraction of a second at her describing the death of her husband as 'unfortunate'. Win some, lose some! But as much as I wanted to pick her theory apart, I knew she was probably right. It's the fear of the unknown that often makes something so powerful, so not knowing for certain whether there was any truth in superstition made it far harder to dispel it.

My biggest achievement in this area was just before I took a flight to Chicago. I saw a penny on the floor as I was about to board, and in that fraction of a second my mind told me to pick it up or the plane would come down. I saw it as my greatest test. I bravely decided to leave it where it was and boarded the plane. The plane crashed. Not really, I was just making sure you were paying attention. I had a smooth flight and my irrational concern was quashed by my ability to see outside of it. It truly was a profound moment for me, but OCD has a wonderful way of flaring up beyond rational measure, and even though this was a huge step forward, I still suffer from the temptation of giving in to irrationality.

The Funny Side of OCD

Everyone who suffers from OCD will experience it differently. Not everyone is obsessed with cleaning. However dark life might seem, sometimes you've just got to see the funny side – like when Rosie developed alopecia but then realised she might never again have to spend money on dry shampoo.

Here's a list of some of my quirky compulsions for LOLs:

■ Kissing the door to avoid death by hellfire.

■ Ensuring all of my stuffed animals can breathe before falling asleep.

■ Making sure the taps are off by singing to them.

■ Never playing music on an odd volume number.

■ Making a small clicking noise with my tongue each time I set an alarm to make sure it's successfully set.

■ Putting my phone on aeroplane mode while I bitch about my friends. Just kidding, LOL . . . Is this thing on?

Understanding mental health disorders is the first step to managing and eventually overcoming them. Looking back at my childhood behaviour, I'm not surprised it manifested so strongly as a teenager. My biggest recurring nightmare as a child involved the White Glove, who was the smartly dressed severed hand of a magician. As an adult I tried to analyse what this could have meant, and came to a number of conclusions. Perhaps it was indicative of my artistic flair and was something I shouldn't ignore; or perhaps it was foresight about always having cold hands due to bad circulation. Either way, I found it terrifying, until the day I confronted it in my unconscious. I shook the hand rather than hiding from it, and it never bothered me again. It's possible that I started having the dream around the same time my parents banned me from watching *The Addams Family*, so perhaps it had something to do with that, I can't be sure. What I am sure of is that by avoiding something, we give it power. So with that being said, the best advice I can offer you is to face your fears and embrace whatever it is that makes you the most uncomfortable. You will reap the biggest rewards.

The one spanner in my works is where spirituality fits into having a condition where being factual and scientific is encouraged to overcome it. If I'm supposed to ignore superstition, am I supposed to ignore my own spiritual beliefs simply because they're not physically tangible or proven? How does religion or religious thinking fit into rational reasoning? I believe in a higher power. An energy far bigger than us that we aren't able to comprehend. Having faith is all about trusting something exists without substantial evidence, so needing to believe that superstition is groundless caused there to be conflict in my mind. It's about finding a balance, and in my experience, there's nothing harder.

Growing up, I was adamantly against religion. I saw it as a power that was being manipulated in order to discriminate rather than to accept. It infuriates me to watch religion being manipulated and abused into control, rather than allowing its true, good essence to flourish. It's taken me years of trying to understand it all, and I'm almost at peace with the idea that I'll never know. But that's exactly one of the lessons having OCD teaches you: being comfortable with uncertainty.

Being 'good' has always been important to me. My mum actually blames *Buffy the Vampire Slayer* for negatively influencing me, and to a certain extent I think she might be right. The show was anchored by a strong theme of good versus evil, and perhaps it affected my development in the sense that I was always looking for a black or white answer. Either way, as an adult I have become far more spiritually awakened. I can't live a life thinking that this is all there is. It very well might be, and I'm not ungrateful for it, but I'm not naive or narcissistic enough to think that we humans understand everything about what we experience in its totality and why it's come to be. Or that we're alone in the universe. If space is infinite, there must be an infinite chance of extraterrestrial life, right?! So the chances are we're going to find it!

I can't help but think that people who say life is life and when you're dead you're dead must fear the possibility that there's something we just can't grasp. This is problematic for the brain to accept, but it's my understanding that energy can be measured but cannot be stopped, only transferred into different energy. That leads me to believe in the possibility of life after death. I'm not saying that when we die we board the cloud tram which terminates at the Pearly Gates, but I can guarantee that everything in my idea of heaven would be parallel and freshly washed. Nah, heaven for me would be even more rudimental than that: a morning when Rosie didn't roll over and exhale her dog breath into my 'strils sounds idyllic.

I believe in angels, and I believe that we all have a divine purpose that we need to recognise and do our best to fulfil. I think my purpose is to help other people who have faced similar struggles through communication and the arts. Or maybe that's wishy-washy orchestrated bullshit and life is in fact purposeless. But that's depressing, and if that was what I believed this book would have been a lot shorter. Even the smallest acts of kindness can turn people's worlds around. Perhaps the meaning of life is to inject moments of happiness into someone else's day so that together we can all make our years here on earth more bearable. What a great responsibility, to have the power to heal people with kindness. In a time when it's so easy to publish your opinions online, when keyboard warriors can remain hidden behind their anonymity, if there's one thing I'll push throughout this book it's to subscribe to our channel . . . but also to treat people kindly. Unless they're dicks with dumbass opinions like 'There's no such thing as global warming.'

For anyone suffering from OCD, anxiety or depression, please trust me when I say that however debilitating, exhausting or impossible it may seem, it doesn't mean you can't achieve every inch of your potential. It'll be a battle that will often seem too great to overcome, but with patience, learning and subscribing to our channel, you'll realise that it's nothing but an impy little bitch. So make it work for you. And when you do, pay it minimum wage.

Everybody Has Quirks

A person who claims to be totally sane is either lying or not very bright. So here's a list of crazy quirks to prove that we all have our issues:

▨ Rosie eats her nostril findings, yet judges me for not taking my cup downstairs after I've used it.

▨ I can't begin any task until the floor is immaculate.

▨ Neither of us can hang up the phone until we've said at least seven consecutive 'byes' to avoid the possibility of an abrupt premature hang up.

▨ Rosie chews food evenly on both sides of her mouth or feels upset.

▨ I believe that polishing something will make it work better and that anything with a scratch is rendered useless.

ROSIE

I have mental health problems. I'm not ashamed to say it, and I don't believe that many of us breeze through life without experiencing any mental health issues whatsoever. I used to be absolutely fine, and now I'm not. And that's OK.

I can pinpoint almost exactly the period in my life when I became 'not fine', and that was during my third year of university. University is when everything got a bit insane for me. The first year was a breeze: all I had to do was pass the year, and none of my grades mattered. I'd met my boyfriend just before I enrolled and I spent a LOT of time raving to my friends about how great he was. He moved into my poky flat with no central heating, and we figured out pretty quickly that it was way too small for both of us, so we moved into a more human-friendly apartment.

Fast-forward to my second year and things were vastly different. My boyfriend broke up with me and moved back in with his mum, leaving me in a bigger flat which I couldn't afford. I started dating Rose and her academic drive both inspired and frightened me. Looking back, it's quite clear that I'd bitten off more than I could chew. My dream was to become a radio presenter, so as well as working at Vue cinema and doing my university work, I also attempted to juggle a weekly radio broadcast, and another job at a different radio station. I also started writing a regular column for a local magazine. I didn't realise it at the time, but I think I was competing with Rose a little bit, and I put a lot of pressure on myself to succeed. Throw in my struggles with my sexuality and having Rose as my first proper lesbian relationship and it's not hard to see why I started freaking out. It was during this second year of uni that I also went through something pretty traumatic, but I wasn't prepared to deal with this until much later, so I pushed it aside in my mind and threw myself into my work and studies.

I was also making YouTube videos with Rose, and some of our

viewers were tuning in to our little local radio show which we broadcast live each week. I began to gain more followers on social media. Through our weekly show, I was offered an internship at a larger radio station, hosting events and running their social media accounts. I can remember starting to panic, the weight of my responsibilities was beginning to drown me. How was I going to keep up with my uni work as well as all these jobs? My peers were not impressed with me getting the internship: the competitive nature of my degree course led to a touch of resentment. I can remember coming into class and finding them all sitting in different seats to usual. It was disappointing to see that they were unable to be happy for me, since we were all working towards a career in media, but my foot was already firmly in the door. For the first time ever in my life I started to care what people thought. Coming into class and hearing people whispering behind me stressed me out, and I became mildly paranoid.

When I look back, it upsets me that I suddenly started to care. I used to be so unfazed by the opinions of others. But I'm also a firm believer in everything happening for a reason. Not caring about other people's opinions can make you a very blunt person. While I gained the feeling of paranoia, I also gained self-awareness, and it taught me a bit more about respecting the feelings of other people. So, in a way, that testing time made me a far more considerate person.

So despite my mounting responsibilities, I took on the internship in the role of of Event Organiser. Because I had to turn up to oversee events, it meant I had to start learning to drive. In the meantime, I was relying on other people – usually Rose, who would have to reschedule her weekend work shifts to ensure I got to where I needed to be.

Everyone wanted me to hurry up and pass my test, so I booked it in much sooner than I should have. While I was practising the day before my test, a car crashed right into the driver's side, and I just lost it. Naturally, after the shock of an incident like that, I failed my test, and I developed alopecia a few weeks afterwards.

This was a total curveball that life threw at me. One morning I woke up, ready to enjoy my day off. I was sat in my kitchen looking at my phone while Rose was making me breakfast, and BOOM. I still don't know how Rose had the guts to tell me that I had a bald patch right on the top of my head. I didn't believe her until I went and looked in the mirror. I immediately booked myself a doctor's appointment, and the doctor I saw will go down in history as one of the worst doctors of all time. He looked me dead in the eye and said, 'You are going to lose all your hair and it will never grow back.' Luckily, neither of those things turned out to be true, but I did continue to go to bed and then mysteriously lose hair during the night. What was mysterious about it was that I never knew where the hair actually went. Another thing the doctor told me was that alopecia was an auto-immune condition. I told him I felt very stressed, and asked if my surprise hair loss could be something to do with that. He said there was no way the two could correlate! How very wrong he was.

I signed up for therapy on the NHS, but in the meantime, my mum recommended I see her friend Sam, who was a trained therapist in Malvern, and I was lucky enough to see her for free. Thus began my first course of therapy.

Let me just pause this story right here and interject with a personal opinion: therapy is fucking awesome. Everybody should have therapy. In a way, sometimes we give each other therapy, simply by listening to each other's problems. There is nothing embarrassing about having therapy or about needing therapy. Everybody in the world has issues, big or small. Also, my therapist had a therapy dog, and that made therapy ten zillion times better. Everything is better with dogs. Everything.

I told Sam that I could never sleep, and with a little further questioning she helped me discover my fear of the dark. I thought she was being silly. She told me to go home, switch on all the lights and try to sleep. I went home. I switched on all the lights. I slept like I was in a coma. We discussed my dad leaving, my sexuality, my family, my relationships, my work life and my car crash. She told me that I was pushing myself way too hard and that I had a fear of failure. I'd put a ridiculous amount of pressure on myself to get first-class honours, and had made myself believe that there was no other option.

With every therapy session, I was waking up having lost less and less hair. Finally, Sam suggested I try beta blockers, and when I started taking them daily, my hair actually started growing back. It was kind of a miracle actually, because most people with alopecia are very lucky if their hair grows back the same – sometimes it can grow back white, or curly, or not at all. The stupid doctor was wrong, and as I overcame my stress and fears my hair loss stopped altogether. There was a direct correlation, and I learned an extremely valuable lesson: your body will do crazy things to let you know there is something wrong.

I stopped my driving lessons and quit my job as Event Organiser for something closer by, with much less mental pressure. I started working at New Look. Although I saw it as a step backwards in my career, I have to admit that it did wonders for my mental health. Working at New Look was easy: you saw clothes on the floor, you hung them up. I made a huge group of girlfriends and my mental health really started to improve.

That was the first time in my life I had mental health issues, and now is the second. So let's talk about my current issues. You guys always want me to tell you a secret, so here it is. I have a tic. A tic is a tiny word for what I consider to be a very annoying, embarrassing and stressful problem.

I first became aware of it when I started dating Rose. She would drive me around in her car and suddenly I would make a noise, or jump, or click, and it would shock her. I didn't really worry too much about it at first, but as time went on, it started to become more frequent. I started to notice that I would shout out words when I didn't mean to. I remember one time Rose and I were on a train to see a musical, and I suddenly shouted a random word out loud. I was hugely embarrassed, and we were sitting opposite a group of boys who all stared at me. Although there wasn't really a way of recovering from that awkward moment, Rose immediately saw the funny side, and we ended up laughing about it for ages.

It soon started to happen more often, and regularly in public. Sometimes it would strike when I was zoned out and not really thinking about anything, like if I was cleaning or showering or getting ready for bed. Sometimes it would happen when I was really busy and had lots on, and I would find myself saying sentences out loud without realising I was saying them. I remember once being in an important meeting, and suddenly feeling so anxious that I would shout out loud.

As well as feeling like I was losing it by uncontrollably shouting, jumping and twitching all the time, I was noticing more and more similarities between my behaviour and Rose's, specifically her OCD compulsions.

For instance, checking. Through YouTube Rose and I are luckily enough to get to travel, and when we go away we check the house, like any normal person does. We check that the doors are locked, that the straighteners aren't on and that the hob is off. These are all normal steps to take to ensure that nothing can catch fire, or that the house is safe from burglary. However, Rose suffers from checking OCD, and could get caught in an exhausting loop of checking something, walking away, doubting herself, and returning to check again. She could sometimes be trapped in this cycle for a long time, and I began noticing that I was doing it too. Before we left the house I would check that every single plug was off, that all the taps were off, that the heating was set correctly, and I would visit every single room to check that it was OK. Then I would do it again, and again.

But unlike Rose, my checking goes further than this, and I have to repeatedly check my handbag. If I was on a train I would check to see if I had everything I needed: my glasses, my purse, my phone. I would check they were there, zip up my bag, then feel a wave of anxiety flood over me, and I would unzip my bag and start the ritual again. I would do this for the duration of the train journey, then check again when I got to my destination. If I took anything out of my bag I would check everything was there again, and sometimes I would make Rose tell me everything that was in my bag in case I didn't check it correctly. Worrying so much over one tiny handbag is nothing compared to packing an entire suitcase, and there have been times when it's made me cry. I am so afraid I will forget to pack something I need, and I write lists and make Rose go over everything I have packed just to triple check, but none of this helps. The worst part is when I hand the airline my luggage and go through security, because then I can't physically check my bag any more.

I know that many of these behavioural patterns can be picked up when living with a partner who suffers from OCD, but I had these ritualistic habits before Rose and I even met. I can remember being fourteen and sitting at the train station checking my bag over and over again, when a friend commented on it and asked what I was so afraid of. The idea of not having what I needed on my person made me physically tremble. I looked it up and checking is actually one of the most common obsessive compulsive behaviours – it's up there with obsessive cleaning.

I was also noticing similarities in the ways that Rose and I ruminate over things. Ruminating, in a nutshell, is thinking deeply about something. But too much thinking can be a bad thing, especially when you go over and over and over the same thought in your brain, over-analysing it, prodding it and allowing it to snowball. Sometimes when this is happening to me Rose can see my eyes glaze over, and she grabs my hand and says, 'Rosie, you're spiralling,' and pulls me back into the real world. I could ruminate or obsess over something for hours, days or even weeks. I ruminate about different things, from wondering whether I said 'thank you' to the cashier who just served me, to spiralling into a full-blown panic attack about something I said to someone years ago.

Recently the tic, the shouting out loud, the over-analysing, the ruminating, the checking all became too much for me to handle. I was exhausted. When I was working, like editing or filming a video, I was OK, but the moment I was left with my own thoughts, I was troubled. I started feeling anxious all the time, over the smallest things, or even experiencing anxiety with no trigger at all. I just wanted to feel safe and comfortable, but for some reason I never felt that way.

I was also starting to feel quite depressed about it all. So I decided it was time for another course of therapy.

I looked up local therapists in my area and what they were qualified to deal with, and found one who looked extremely promising, and not just because of her resemblance to Jean Holloway in *Gypsy*. I could have popped down to my GP and got referred, but fortunately, for the first time in my life, I had the money to pay for private care. The only reason I did this was because I felt that I needed to be seen right away, before my mental health plummeted even further. Despite my high opinion of free available healthcare, it's a shame the NHS can't always see people that quickly.

Although it was awkward and embarrassing telling a stranger my problems, I was impressed with my new therapist's reaction. I was also impressed with the comedy-sized iPad Pro that she was taking notes on – that thing looked great and I had professional equipment envy. From our first session she told me that I had issues with safety. I asked her if she thought I had OCD and she said, 'Yes, but we have to work out *why* it is that you are doing these things.' Then she blew my mind with a concept. She told me that she didn't think my tic was the usual tic when someone has an involuntary vocal or physical behaviour. She said she thought I was shouting out as part of suffering from post-traumatic stress disorder, and suggested I have eye movement desensitisation and reprocessing (EMDR) therapy to cope.

Although it felt overwhelming to spill out all my secrets to someone other than Rose (I hadn't even discussed any of my problems with my family), I felt hopeful that together we had made a plan, and I really began to trust my therapist.

Next on the agenda was to create a 'trauma timeline', to figure out the things that might be upsetting me. How funny that though I was clearly very troubled and upset by things in my past, I didn't know what they were. My therapist had told me that even lots of tiny upsetting events can contribute to post-traumatic stress disorder.

Life happened in a way that meant I wasn't able to see my therapist for a few weeks, so I had a great deal of time on my hands to think about this trauma timeline. But I didn't write it. I kept putting it off. Obviously there was something I was just not ready to confront. In the end, Rose wrote down my trauma timeline for me, as I was finding it too difficult to face. She didn't presume to know more about my life than I did, she just said she would write down the things that she knew had been traumatic for me, and if I wanted to add or remove something, obviously that was up to me. We talked through the timeline she'd drawn up and it was only then, years and years after the actual event, that I finally confronted something I had been through during my second year of university. I was raped.

I won't go into any more detail because it's triggering and unpleasant to discuss. But what I will say is that I was only two or three sessions into my therapy and I was already getting to the root of my problems. I googled 'post-traumatic stress disorder' and realised that I had every one of the symptoms listed. I also started researching other people's mental health reactions after sexual assaults, and related so much to other people's stories. Therapy was helping me realise what my issues were, that I wasn't alone and how to cope.

I actually had my first session of EMDR therapy yesterday. It was tough, and not just because my hot therapist was wearing quite a short dress. I had to hold these little plastic things in my hands (I know, I'm excellent at descriptions, LOL) and the plastic thingies would flash a little light one at a time, and I had to follow the light with my eyes. So I would be looking left, then right, then left, like watching a tennis match. I had to take myself back to a painful memory and tell my therapist my thought process, while my eyes followed the flashes. I was really getting into it, despite the fact that I had snot dripping down my face, which I couldn't wipe away because I was still holding the plastic things. I had to imagine I was back in that traumatic moment, and I could feel every bit of hurt and anger and disappointment like it was happening again. And then my therapist dropped her iPad stylus on the floor. I had to try to keep my eyes tracking the lights but in my peripheral view I could see that she was trying to reach the stylus with the heel of her shoe, which I found funny and mildly seductive. I tried to remain in the moment and keep going – until she actually bent down and crawled under her desk to retrieve the stylus in THAT dress. So overall I'd say that my first EMDR therapy was a success and that I'm looking forward to my next session . . . despite crying so intensely that I came home missing a nose stud!

As I'm still currently undergoing therapy I can't tell you how this chapter in my life will end, but it's already beginning to get a little better. In 2016 Kylie Jenner said that it was the year of 'realising stuff', and that's how I feel right now. With therapy I have realised a LOT of stuff. Why I behave the way I do, why I think the way I think, and what all that might mean. I sometimes wish I could have realised it all back in 2K16 like Kylie did, but Rose reminded me that most people have some kind of crisis in their life at least once, and we can't all go through it at the same time because that would be carnage.

Something I know I do wrong, which I am trying to fix, is being too hard on myself. I've seen a lot of people I know do this, too. Sometimes you are your own worst critic. I might berate myself for not working hard enough, not completing my tasks for the day, or not immediately clapping back with an excellent retort. On the one hand it's amazing: I'm a pusher and I push myself to be the best I can be in all areas of my life. On the other hand, I give myself unrealistic expectations and then punish myself for not living up to these impossible standards. Another thing I'm totally shit at is giving myself any sort of praise. I do something right, and I move on. I know I need to make more of an effort to celebrate even my smaller feats.

But it's not all bad. Everyone has problems and mine are hardly the worst. I have definitely experienced anxiety, and I am unlucky enough to have been on the receiving end of a few unforgettable panic attacks. I can remember, as if it was yesterday, the first panic attack I ever had, and it was about losing Rose. We had an argument and we couldn't reach an agreement, and I thought to myself, *This is it, it's going to end and I don't want it to end but it has to end* . . . and before I knew it I was gone, lost in the void of what-ifs. More recently, I had a totally unfounded and irrational panic attack that I would lose the use of my legs. I made myself so ill that I took off all my clothes and sat there naked, just trying to get some air into my lungs. It was about 3 a.m. and I left sweat patches on the bed. Now I can look back at that and laugh. But just because something is stupid and irrational in hindsight, it doesn't mean you can't panic about it at the time.

Coping Mechanisms

I've definitely picked up a fair few tricks on how to cope with anxiety, panic attacks and problems in general. It goes without saying that what works for me might not work for somebody else, but here are a few ways I have managed to heal myself.

MEDITATION

A big reliever for me has been meditation, even if it's just for three minutes a day. I use the free version of the Headspace app (no, this isn't #spon. You buying the book was amazing enough!), and I go particularly crazy with this before I do a live event – it helps create a small gap in time between the persistent dashes to the toilet!

LESS CAFFEINE

Despite my serious addiction to caffeine, I have found that when one is overburdened, lessening your caffeine intake does wonders, as does a huge glass of cold water, or a wonderful chamomile tea.

JOURNALLING

One thing my first therapist taught me was to keep a diary, even if you just scribble random words in it. I used to journal every single night before bed without fail, and it's a foolproof method of getting things off your mind . . . and into Rose's. I dump my thoughts onto paper and leave them there, allowing space for beautiful dreams and a tranquil sleep.

ROUTINE

My therapist taught me the value of a good routine, to get some wind-down time before bed to allow your mind to take a break for a bit. Unfortunately I'm not too great at following my own advice, so my good routine has flown out the window. But it was great while it lasted and I strongly recommend to anyone who has trouble sleeping that a hot bath and a good, but semi-boring book before bed can work wonders.

I understand that all of the tips above are probably common

knowledge and are stuff your grandma might have said to you. I also understand that when struggling with mental health issues, a nice bath, good sleep and a good book are not the cure to all your problems. But what I will say is that sometimes people say things like 'Make sure you drink enough water' so often that you end up ignoring it. But try not to forget that sometimes the small, simple things can really help, and that your grandma says them for a reason!

I'm also learning a lot about self-care, and this is where the internet and, more importantly, you guys come in. I have been vocal about my anxiety, speaking about it in a few vlogs and also on Twitter. The amazing part of having an audience is the huge response you can get to any question or problem raised. You guys have linked me to calming websites, breathing exercises, relaxing games – you name it, you've recommended it. Rose and I are also part of many group chats on Twitter, and you guys are incredibly supportive and are always reminding Rose and me to rest, not to work too hard and to drink plenty of water. I really appreciate people taking the time out to give me tips and helpful comments, so thank you. I can honestly say that you have truly helped.

In fact, there's nothing wrong with asking for help. I have sometimes written on Twitter that I am feeling a bit down, and my friends have immediately texted me. I don't know why, but it always surprises me how kind and considerate people are. You might also be surprised when other people know exactly how you're feeling and have some helpful advice. One thing I'm beginning to learn is that you are truly not alone. Whatever problem you are suffering with, there is someone else out there suffering with the same issue. This thought has brought me comfort, because no one wants to feel totally isolated and alone.

Discussing my mental health problems with Rose has only deepened our bond. In fact, it has made me even more certain in my belief that Rose and I are meant to be together. Her ability to understand exactly how I'm feeling is so comforting, and some of the hurdles I'm facing Rose has already been through herself.

I've met people who have OCD and they have told Rose and me that seeing our relationship is inspiring, because they worry that having OCD will make them difficult to love, or strenuous to live with. They see Rose and me living happily together and that gives them hope.

When Rose and I started dating she told me she suffered from OCD, that she had been clinically diagnosed and had attended both group and one-to-one therapy. She told me a few of the things she used to do in childhood, and some I related to and others I didn't. Rose used to have the compulsion to kiss the door of her downstairs bathroom each time she passed the threshold. She was obsessed that something bad would happen, and routinely kissed the door to cancel out the possibility of a negative outcome. In her mind, this was perfectly rational.

I find her obsessions and compulsions fascinating, cute and a part of her. Rose wouldn't be Rose without her OCD. But please do not think I am trivialising her problems when I call them cute. I've been with her during some of her worst OCD episodes, and I understand and have witnessed how physically and emotionally hard and heartbreaking it is for her. But together we can also see the funny side!

Rose has an obsession with clean floors and vacuums the same patch of floor about fifty times a day. We could be desperately late and about to miss a train and Rose will be shouting, 'Hurry, Rosie, let's go!' while simultaneously vacuuming the problem area that's already as clean as it possibly could be. She buys antibacterial wipes and gets on her hands and knees to give it the attention it deserves. I can see that it's tiring, and that she'd rather be doing something else, but she has the compulsion to do it and it has to be done.

She will have to tidy the house from top to bottom before she brings anything new into it. For instance, if we were to get a new laptop for work, the entire house must be 'perfect' for her to allow this new item to enter our space. She will have to clean the house in its entirety before she starts a new game on the PlayStation, like *The Sims*. Rose's dream is to make it to a third generation of *The Sims*, playing the same family. The reason she has never accomplished this is because she will feel the family is no longer perfect and has to start all over again.

Rose's obsession with perfection is something I love and admire about her. I believe it's the reason we are so successful. Her drive is sexy: I love how she wakes up every morning bursting with creativity and ideas and wants to get stuck in. It gives her so much energy, although sometimes her need for perfection involves staying up editing until 3 a.m. because she doesn't want to go to bed with an unfinished project. I love her need for perfection, I love how she wants her surroundings to be perfect, her work to be perfect . . . but people can't be perfect.

To the people who suffer, whether it's with OCD or another issue, and worry that this makes you 'unlovable', please stop worrying. I can assure you that I have never once thought, *I really wish Rose didn't have OCD*, or, *Rose's OCD really makes me hate living with her.* The people who love you accept you for exactly who you are. Rose and I strive to lift each other up when it comes to our issues, and I cannot sing Rose's praises enough when it comes to how supportive she is. She has the time to talk through any concern of mine, and she never has any judgement. She doesn't care whether it's a small, petty point or something deep and life-changing. She never makes me feel guilty if I'm sad or down and she actively tells me off if I ever apologise. Everyone has the right to feel the way they feel.

The only downside to living with Rose and her OCD is that we can accidentally 'feed' each other's compulsions. For example, Rose likes to have the volume of the car radio on an even number. Her OCD tells her that something will go wrong and the car will crash otherwise. I used to help her challenge this compulsion and would deliberately set the volume to an odd number, to prove that the numbers on the dial do not affect her driving ability. However, as time passed, I also started wanting the numbers on an even setting. We can both sink into bad habits if we let ourselves, and this is something we definitely need to nip in the bud.

I would like to mention that Rose has had years of different kinds of therapy and still suffers from OCD. She has accepted that she will always suffer from it, because it is a part of her. However, she can live with it now because she has the understanding and the coping mechanisms to do so. I am having therapy and am confronting a lot of pain and trauma from my past which is still affecting my present. I don't expect to never feel pain when I think of these traumatic moments, but I want to learn to be able to sit with myself and feel OK. It's a goal I am working towards.

But when I reflect, I realise that these problems Rose and I suffer with haven't prevented us from living our lives. We met, we fell in love, we got married. We've just bought our first house. We are doing a job we love. We're writing a book! So if you're going through something, I want you to know that there is so much hope, and there are so many wonderful things to come for you.

There are times when I still feel sad; I have some days when I can't do anything because I feel so down. But on a dog walk the other day, Rose said to me, 'Think of the worst times in your life. Did you notice that no matter how bad you felt, the sun kept rising and the world kept turning?' This made me feel so relieved. She was right, obviously! Every day is a new day. Every day can be an improvement on the last if you try. Even when I'm upset and suffering, I still have moments when I laugh, or feel so happy or in love. I still have goals and aims and dreams. I urge you not to give up, because it truly does get better.

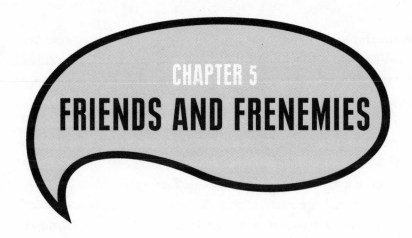

CHAPTER 5
FRIENDS AND FRENEMIES

'My friendship circle is more of a line.'

ROSE

Friends are a huge part of life. They shape you, they support you, they lift you up. Mine have been pivotal in their positive contribution to my mental health, and even though I can count my close friends on one hand, I'd take that over a dozen who are only friends at face value.

I'm not too keen on burning bridges when it comes to friendships. I think it's fair to say that Rosie burns bridges, collects the charred remains and displays them as wall art, and even though I respect her approach, it's not usually the way I work. I'm a believer in fighting for a relationship, but that doesn't mean you have to accept friendships that aren't positive for you.

As I reluctantly approach my thirtieth year as an earthling, I've realised my social circle is actually more of a line. A line that connects me to Rosie. I used to worry that my tight-knit friendship group was unravelling and that the reason was my odour or because of flaws in my personality, but I've come to realise it's both. I'm lying, but sometimes I think it would be easier to have a straightforward explanation as to why friends disappear. I would tell myself that the only reason my circle of friends was getting smaller was because we'd all drifted apart, were living in different parts of the world, and had careers that were wildly different from one another. And despite all those things being true, there was still something in the paranoid region of my temporal lobe that hinted at the possibility that the real reason was me.

Growing up, I always had a socially awkward disposition. When I was six I was mentally traumatised at a National Trust location for touching the exhibit. The telling-off I received for reaching beyond the red rope had a profound effect on my development. It prevented me from reaching out to people emotionally, in fear there was a line I shouldn't cross. Even though that statement's dramatically untrue, it's also believable. One should never underestimate a child's ability to carry shame. But some things I did take away from that embarrassing public experience were a trigger for my social anxiety: a blunt gift-shop pencil sharpener, and the knowledge that period manors are not child-appropriate, since you can't touch or lick anything.

As a result of NationalTrustgate, I'm extremely sensitive to anything other than effortless, smooth social interaction and so I will go out of my way to try to achieve it. I'll fill any silence to avoid a painful momentary pause and will bring as much energy to a conversation as possible. No need to meet me halfway, I'm always prepared to go the full distance and will even pack my own lunch. I'm very emotionally in tune with myself and with other people, I pick up on tone and tact, and I strive for nothing less than perfect conversational synergy. So what's changed recently?

Maybe I've just started to give less fucks, or maybe I'm too busy to feel I need to take full responsibility for every conversation I have. Either way, I've noticed that I'm starting to pull back a bit and not always be the one who makes the most effort or goes the extra mile. Friendships are a two-way street, not a one-way road, and it's important to build them properly to avoid potholes and pitfalls. Like romantic relationships they take work, honesty, understanding, compromise, compassion and patience. But all of that sounds really time-consuming and potentially a little gay, doesn't it? I'm not sure if I can be bothered either! It's not that I don't want friends, I just don't want to go to the ends of the earth for them and then realise they weren't worth it. The amount of time I've spent going the distance thinking my efforts would be matched is time I could have spent snacking or inventing renewable energy. I know you shouldn't buy someone a birthday present with the expectation of one in return, but let's be honest, what's more satisfying than giving? Receiving. That's what Christmas is all about and it's the message I plan to impart to my children.

ROSIE

I like to think that I have a talent for making new friends, but unfortunately my talent sometimes fails me when it comes to making the right ones. This simply reflects my lack of forward thinking, and I'm always getting myself into situations I struggle to get out of. I've had a multitude of friends over the years and have learned myriad lessons because of it. I've learned not to get too excited about someone too quickly, and not to share my secrets with the first person I meet but to save them, put them in a book and make a profit. In this chapter I want to go through some examples of my over-zealous self getting too caught up in someone then instantly regretting it. Basically I've made the mistakes so you don't have to.

First, there was Kathy. Kathy was the new girl at school. My form tutor asked who wanted to show her around and I eagerly raised my hand. I walked over to meet her at reception and there she was. How can I say this without being mean? Kathy was scary. First of all, she was German – which is absolutely fine, just not what I was expecting. Secondly, her unanticipated and unshake-able interest in me later led me to believe that Kathy was in love with me. I was taken aback by Kathy. But being the type of person who doesn't dismiss possible relationships based on bad haircuts and a possible culture clash, I was still keen to start a friendship! We walked around school together, Kathy bounding alongside me panting, '*Oh ja!*'

It was all well and good until the tour had ended and I realised I couldn't shake her off, not even to dash to the toilet. There was no break from Kathy. I found her in all my classes, sitting dutifully beside me. I was beginning to get used to her ginger curls in my peripheral vision.

Kathy invited me round to her house and I discovered two things: one, that her mother was also too much; and two, that Kathy and I had nothing in common. Initially, listening to the German translation for every household object was fairly close to fun, but after a couple of hours I was tired, bored and increasingly concerned I'd never see my family again. In school I tried to distance myself a little and managed to hide for a lesson or two, until Kathy found me again, with her big watery eyes, and asked me if we were still friends. 'Of course!' I yelled. I was trapped for ever.

This leads me on to Donna Kebab. Her name was Donna, so naturally people called her Donna Kebab. I've never had one myself but I'm sure they're quite lovely. We struck up a friendship when a supply teacher unfairly picked on her for her make-up choices. I was livid that a temporary, nobody excuse of a teacher dared question Donna's choice of blue eyeshadow. The supply teacher was lecturing us on how make-up should 'enhance NATURAL beauty' and I loudly remarked that a make-up detour wasn't the natural way to enhance the lesson. Donna appreciated this and we started sitting together in lessons and I realised she was incredibly funny!

The warning bells started ringing on an after-school trip to Donna's house. On the bus, Donna got out her lighter and started to set fire to the seat in front of us. The driver stopped the bus and yelled at us for the impromptu arson. I didn't appreciate the humiliation; it wasn't pleasant. Then we got to Donna's house, which didn't have a door. Donna offhandedly explained that it had been kicked in by thugs. Then she told me to 'hide my school tie so we don't get beaten up' on our trip to the park. I got a bitter taste in my mouth, and not just from the second-hand smoke from Donna's menthol cigarettes. The final straw was when we went to the shops and I detected Donna's breezy penchant for shoplifting. After that I was out, and my giggles in the classroom with Donna were no more.

Like Kathy, this bad decision-making pattern followed me around for years. It became clear to me that my problem lay not only at the beginning of these ill-fated friendships but also at the ending of them. I just didn't know how to. It's fair to say that some people are not right for us and it's natural for relationships and friendships to end occasionally. People come into our lives for a reason or a season, but if it's true that you have to go through a few bad eggs to get to the good ones, it's no wonder I went vegan!

ROSE

Kathy, if you're reading this, I'd very much appreciate an introduction to German via household items. Knowledge is power.

It's funny how adulthood has taught me to be able to predict where a friendship is going. There have been a few people who have actively distanced themselves from me because it's preferable for them not to have ask about the things Rosie and I are doing. You have to remember that Rosie and I are from very small towns, and in the grand scheme of YouTube we're by no means superstars, but anyone who's actually moved out of the Shire borders is deemed spirited if not valiant. If you defeat the river troll at Lower Lydbrook to pass beyond the perimeter of the forest, you'll be awarded two wives and a talisman for your bravery and onward journey. So please don't think I'm blowing my own boar tusk when I raise the possibility of friends being jealous.

It's difficult when that happens, but it's balanced out by the few amazing friends who've changed my life for ever! These friends came to me when I needed them the most, just as I was recovering from my OCD and was anxiously back in education. Can you call art college education? I'm unsure. Our days were spent playing travel chess, learning substandard parkour, and seeing how many art supplies we could steal undetected. Tom, Emma and Bliv were the three people who brought me out of my shell, who had zero judgement of my mental health, my bad skin or confused fashion sense. They allowed me to be myself even before I really knew who that was. Being surrounded by uplifting, happy and supportive people gave me the foundation I needed to grow. I really owe everything to them. I'd never felt so safe and secure in my own skin. Even if it was covered in acne! These were the types of friends who could immediately take the power out of any concern. They were able to make jokes about any worry I had, until that worry became so insignificant it barely existed. These relationships taught me never to settle for anyone who doesn't accept you for everything that you are. Because even if you don't love yourself yet, others will, and they can help you discover parts of yourself you never even thought of celebrating.

Friends like these come once in a lifetime. I don't see them often, but when I do I'm eighteen again. Whether we're joking about dropping Tom's kids, leaving tips in a foreign currency, or reminiscing about the old days, I'm proud of their successes and I know they're proud of mine. And that's what true friendship's about! Not resenting people for the things they have or the places they've been, but being happy for them! Tom and his wife Lauren have three beautiful children. Am I jealous of their family? No. Did I offer to buy one of his kids? Yes. But as a friend, I accepted his refusal to sell his baby on moral grounds. That's called 'understanding'.

I think it's good to rise above things and not let pettiness get the better of you. However, everyone has that one thing they can't let go of. (I'm still angry that Tara was killed off so brutally in *Buffy* season 6, although I've tried to make peace with the fact that her death was the narrative catalyst for Willow's dark-arts demise.) In general I try not to bear grudges, but I'm sure we all have one person from school we'd love to get one over on. That can actually be the best motivation to achieve your goals – like in the aftermath of a bad break-up – as you strive to achieve more in the race to smug face. I am guilty of this – I'm human, I'm guilty of a lot of things. Like flawlessness.

A few years ago we were in a very tricky position. We were given the opportunity to fly to Singapore to interview Tom Hanks, Ron Howard, Melissa McCarthy and Paul Feig. So when this opportunity fell into our laps we were totally over the moon. The drama arose when it clashed with a friend's wedding in England, leaving us in the position of having to explain why we'd be unable to attend the wedding. Perhaps you're thinking that good friends would have sacrificed the trip and if that had been you, you'd have put your friend first. I get that. But we didn't grow up together, we'd never worked together and we'd never shared X Factor-style sob stories. So it wasn't like I was letting down an inseparable childhood tie, and I felt no moral obligation to attend other than the fact we'd already agreed to.

This wasn't a last-minute cancellation in the slightest. Rosie and I gave her four months' notice. I expected her to be disappointed, and I didn't feel great about prioritising an opportunity over her big day. But what I DID NOT expect was an itemised bill of expenses our cancellation would incur. When I got married even some of my cousins didn't attend at the last minute. I didn't send them a bill. (I sent river trolls because it's the only way I know how to communicate.)

It was a little awkward asking if she wanted compensation for our cancellation 122 days prior to the event, but she assured me that she was simply highlighting the consequences of our cancellation rather than explicitly asking to be reimbursed for her losses. I didn't know how our friendship was going to bounce back from this. I thought about sending her the cost of a wedding gift I was yet to buy to highlight the potential expense our cancellation would incur, but was told this was unnecessarily argumentative. Even so, I was unsure as to why our places would cost her anything at this stage, or why they couldn't be just filled by other guests, but these were questions I was going to have to live with. Like never knowing why humans don't just sniff other humans the way dogs do, so we can quickly make an assessment whether or not to pursue a relationship based on butt smell.

Something I really value in my good friends is their ability to interact – sounds simple, but it's funny how many people don't adhere to the basic rules of engagement! A few months ago Rosie and I met up with a friend for a long-awaited catch-up. This friend also happened to be a YouTuber, so it was great to have the opportunity to talk about things they'd understand as another creator. We spent a laborious afternoon listening. About twenty minutes in I was resigned to the fact that I wasn't going to be asked a single question. No, 'But how are you guys?' Or, 'Haven't you got a UK tour coming up?' Or even, 'Do you want to hear more about my everyday breakfast routine?' I didn't, but the opportunity to answer something would have been nice. How do people socialise this way without thinking the conversation is completely one-sided? I don't understand it, especially since I'm so careful not to dominate a conversation and will always ask about the other person first.

Perhaps this is a good opportunity to list some of the qualities I'm looking for in a friend, followed by everything a friend can expect from me.

What I Expect from a Friend

■ Willing to sing the chorus on days when I decide life's a musical.

■ Would raise my children if I got bored.

■ Would sacrifice an organ even if I didn't need it, just wanted it.

■ Would encourage my breakthroughs in medicine by participating as a test subject.

■ Willing to do time.

What a Friend Can Expect from Me

■ Getting the bill. I can't let other people pay or even split the bill because I find it so uncomfortable.

■ Honesty.

■ Presents from John Lewis.

■ My last M&M.

■ My undivided attention when I have time.

■ A platter of antipasti upon arrival.

ROSIE

Jealousy is something I've had to learn a lot about when it comes to friends. As someone who is naturally enthusiastic about the good things happening in other people's lives, I find it hard to even conceive that someone could possibly be jealous of us, and if I'm quite frank, I think letting jealousy get the better of you makes you a weak person. It's not that hard to smile at someone and compliment them on something they are proud of, whether or not you consider them 'deserving' of their good fortune.

But if you think I'm about to let a few Negative Nancys ruin my happiness, you're wrong. I don't do my daily gratitude lists for nothing! A good friend will share your delight about anything that you're even slightly passionate about, because a good friend finds enthusiasm contagious! They care about your feelings, your life events; they want to help, to listen, to share it all with you. I don't expect perfection from a friend – no one is a mind reader or can be pleased for you 24/7. But I do expect to be treated exactly as I treat others: I wish them the best, and I encourage their happiness.

ROSE

Deciding to let go and draw a line under a friendship can be one of the toughest decisions to make. I wish I could say that I had a friend left from high school, but the truth is I don't. I never made strong connections there, and my memories of it aren't fond. Popularity is an ever-changing concept. Its requirements have changed so dramatically over the years, and yet some things have remained the same. Talking about your issues was never something that was widely accepted, and there was always an overbearing element of shame that surrounded open discussion. Whether it be sexual orientation or mental health, back in school I never felt able to share these things without running the risk of being labelled as different and branded unpopular. And even though it can still be incredibly difficult for kids, teenagers and even adults to open up, even in a safe, non-judgemental environment, I think there's a lot more acceptance and widespread support now than there once was.

People bash the online community for its trolls and its hate speech, but from what I've seen it's proved to be one of the most supportive communities available to us. Popularity no longer solely hinges on appearing 'cool', with all of its superficial values. It can come from just being yourself. Many people online have been brave enough to publicly expose themselves, at the same time tapping into a lot of the insecurities that many of us struggle with, and providing us with someone to relate to. They become a voice for those who don't feel they have one and offer comfort to those who seek it. If you look at most incredibly successful YouTubers, a lot of them have been and remain very vocal on issues they struggle with. Anxiety, eating disorders, gender identity or mental health – talking about these things at school wasn't even an option for me. So it's great to see this positive movement helping so many people! If there'd been a YouTuber who spoke about suffering with OCD back when I needed it, I would have watched every single one of their videos.

But there's a flip side to everything so let's get real for a second. Popularity online is *also* based on looks, clothes, cars, staged photographs and items of high material value. We're all guilty of editing our lives to appear more enriched, and I'm not going to sit here and pretend I'm above all that because I have a compulsion to be honest. I'm no exception, I absolutely apply filters! I absolutely try out every one before uploading to Instagram. Is it shameful to want to look your 'best'? Well, here's the thing: there is a big difference between wanting to look your best online and editing your entire life story. Even though we all do it to a certain degree, there are friends of mine who go above and beyond. Friends from school, friends from work, other influencers, all in a constant battle for the most impressive experience, the cutest love story, the most thrilling adventure. We look at their photographs and think, *Damn, they're truly living their best life. Why aren't I doing that? I need to up my game. I need to get out there, or better yet, I need to APPEAR like I'm out there* . . . It's tough not to get consumed by it and conform when everyone else seems to be!

But what I've realised is that 'popularity' has nothing to do with true friendship. Yes, it's nice to feel liked, to feel popular, and it's also nice to appear like you're having a fantastic life! But friendships should never be based on how successful you are or how pretty, how wealthy or how adventurous you seem. The friendships that last are the friendships based on your truth. You should never feel obligated to lie or exaggerate to appeal to someone. If that's what impresses them the most, rather than the intrinsic person you are, then perhaps they're not the right friends for you. I realise it's very easy to tell you to try not to worry about the way you come across online, in a world where our online profile is fast becoming the first thing other people are introduced to. But keep in mind that you're more than your bio and your profile picture, and so are other people.

Although I'm certainly one to apply a filter, one thing I've never done is misled my audience into thinking I'm happier, more wild, or more in love than I am in real life. I treat Instagram like my own photo journal to document the places I've been and the happy occasions in my life. With the exception of an occasional ad, all of the photographs I upload would be the same even if no one was following me. Try to remain as true to yourself as possible. Then you remove the pressure to be anything other than yourself.

ROSIE

How could I talk about friendship without mentioning Facebook, the very founder of the term 'friend request'. I find Facebook and the different ways people use it totally *fascinating*. The bragging, the ranting statuses – I don't know what I loathe the most. Actually I do: it's the humblebrag!

Now, as a young person working in social media, I understand that the very essence of social media is self-indulgence. Everyone wants to portray their best side to the world online, and of course there's nothing wrong with that. If I have the choice of a photo taken from a bad angle or one with a flattering pose and a sexy filter, I know which one I'd choose for my profile pic.

But I *am* judging the social-media braggers. Here are a few classic examples of social-media bragging that I love to hate!

■ People who check in to first-class lounges on Facebook. Even worse, the people who pretend to be taking a casual selfie, but position something within shot in a totally orchestrated pose that clearly took fifty-five tries to get right that makes it obvious they're in first class.

■ People who talk about how busy they are in a failed attempt to act overwhelmed, when they are really just trying to show off their high-profile, jam-packed itinerary and rubbing your full-time, no-holiday-days-left nose in it.

■ Mothers who use their baby to create a 'baby flat lay', much like bloggers do with their breakfast in a hotel room post. No one cares how old your baby is this week.

■ People who upload every single photo they took on their three-month long trip to Bali. I don't need to see 550 photos of you in the same outfit next to the same elephant. I. DON'T. CARE.

■ And finally, the cherry on this over-inflated cake is the multi-item money shot. This is when a person has a lot of money and has spent it on many high-price material posses-sions. They want to show off said possessions but don't know where to begin – or perhaps they do want everything in one shot, to make the most impact. Either way, the result is this: the most uncomfortable staged photo that typically consists of a Mercedes, a coffee cup clasped in a manicured hand with an expensive engagement/wedding ring, a swanky watch, and a fixed smile revealing whitened pegs. This one is honestly my favourite, especially the version where someone else has had to take the photo in order to capture both jewellery-laden hands clasping the steering wheel. The lengths some people will go to online to flaunt money is priceless.

So, guys – why do some people do this? Why all the passive aggression and self-importance? When did Facebook turn into such a competition? I'm guessing the cut-throat gloating began shortly after people woke up to social media's dark side: as a mechanism to stalk old flames and former friends. We've all been there, and sometimes we get caught doing it, but that still doesn't stop us. Once while checking out my ex-boyfriend's Instagram page, my greasy digits slipped clumsily and I accidentally liked one of his photos. Even worse, I didn't realise, so the photo remained liked. I went off to work, and then my ex screenshotted my like and UPLOADED MY HORRIFIC MISTAKE TO HIS INSTAGRAM. He smugly and publicly called me out on my humiliatingly blatant investigation, and it was broadcast on his page for the world to see.

But why was I getting all private detective on my ex in the first place? I know why. I wanted to know what he was up to, and perhaps I wanted to see if I was doing better than him. Please don't judge me because I'm sure you can all relate to my honesty. Who doesn't want to have the upper hand, especially over someone who spectacularly dumped you? I suppose this admittedly narcissistic viewpoint is the exact reason why some people show off on social media.

While we're being so decent and honest, who hasn't checked up on some people from their past, or even their present? The only way I'm still connected to most of my school friends is through Facebook, and there is something addictively compelling about observing a bunch of people who grew up together, and then all went their separate ways to live totally different lives.

Here are a few clichéd but totally honest observations from a quick perusal of old school peers on my personal Facebook:

Lots of people have babies now.

That's it.

Does it make me feel good to check up on people? Not really; it's not something I do often, but I'd be lying if I said I'd never done it. Do I revel in glee when I can see someone has drawn the short straw in life? Absolutely not. We've all been through our low points, and social media has almost certainly documented them. What about when someone is doing well? Then I'm genuinely happy for them! Which I suppose makes the whole concept of checking up on people rather redundant, if you are only going to empathise with their unhappiness or congratulate their success. I suppose the moral of the story would be: don't do it. Don't Facebook stalk your past or present peers, exes, work colleagues or friends of friends. Just don't.

But here's a delightful concept, that I hope will make me appear wise rather than old and past it. There is more to life than how well you are doing in comparison to everyone else. There is more to life than how many likes you get on a post or status. You are more than your social media profiles. Ask yourself this: how many people on your Facebook would you actually call a friend? Now ask yourself this: who cares? Is anyone really looking at you that closely? And if they are, perhaps they should be focusing more on their own habits.

ROSE

One of my biggest motivations was wanting to do better than the losers at school who'd looked down on me because I didn't think drugs were cool. I mean, what *wasn't* cool about numbing their crippling insecurity while dressed as something from a *Matrix* fan convention? And as sad as it is, nothing is more satisfying than seeing what they're up to now when they try to add me as a friend on Facebook. You didn't speak to me in school, I've had no contact with you since then, but fourteen years later, you decide now is the time to reach out? Well, guess what, I'm not a National Trust exhibit you assume you can reach out to.

So what do I do when this happens? I accept their friend request. You might be thinking, *Hold up, you've lost me*, but let me explain the sheer deliciousness. I accept their friend request for twenty-four hours, to allow them enough time to peruse my photographs, see the places I've been to and the achievements Rosie and I have accomplished together, so they know that their rebuffing of my high-school social advances has had no effect on my life. I let that sink in overnight while I scroll through their colourful employment history. Now, I'm not a job snob – how could I be when most people assume I'm 'lucky' to have the job I do? But when I see unsavoury high-school characters from the past trying to dress up their job title for the sake of social media, my mouth waters. That's my drug. How ironic that the high I get is from seeing how they've never evolved or amounted to anything. What poetry!

After a twenty-four-hour window of analysis I delete them. It's what I like to call the old 'add and destroy'. Let them experience the dopamine surge of an accepted request, only to deprive them of it later. That is so messed up I can't even believe I just wrote it . . . I can't believe how GENIUS it is! Don't get me wrong, I'm not really full of bitterness and resentment, because I don't think negative emotions can ever be the sole driving force propelling you to achieve something positive. They can act as the springboard, but you have to take yourself the whole way because you want it for *you*. (Just thought I'd add that bullshit sentence to appear enlightened. Nailed it!)

I always thought adult friendships would work differently to childhood ones, and although they're far more passive aggressive in terms of bragging or fighting without actually arguing, the emotional neediness is exactly the same, we just display it differently. We think we're cleverer than we were as children, masking our emotions, appearing unbothered, or communicating with passive aggression rather than honesty. But not everyone is like this. Rosie is so pure that she's totally unable to adopt the characteristics of the City Serpent.

Serpentine behaviour predominantly manifests in a form of communication that stems from both an attacking and a defensive position. I call it serpenting. Serpents strive to catch you out, whether that's in a lie, by manipulating, or simply in an attempt to defend themselves. I'm extremely good at serpenting because it's the way my family communicates. I was raised in a nest. Laura, my mother and I would argue through tactical passive-aggressive strikes, and even though we all knew we were arguing, we never admitted to it. That was conceding and it meant you were out of the game. It was a battle of who could strategically corner the other person first, a war of words, like lawyers desperate to keep a cool head but salivating at the thought of their next blow.

Serpenting is like an ice-cold bitch slap that's intended to highlight the weaknesses in your argument. It's the way we communicate in business, where the art is to win without appearing emotional. What's ironic is that there's nothing clever or 'adult' about arguing in fluent serpent with your friends or family. When two people are stripped back, have an honest conversation and just say what's upsetting them, things are quickly resolved and everyone can move forward without the laborious game-playing. But that's not as fun, is it? And it's certainly not in my nature. Why be honest when you can dance around your point for hours? It's like Monopoly: why go for Park Lane when you could dominate the entire street leading up to it? Nothing beats the satisfaction of knowing you've won before actually winning.

I'll never forget my first lesson in Serpent Key Stage 1. My mum picked me up from primary school and as we were walking back to where she'd parked, my friend William zipped past in the new family car he'd spent all day bragging about. He was sitting in the back seat as his mother revved the N-reg so we'd all turn to look. As I did so, William threw me a smug glance and a facetiously slow wave. My face turned to thunder, I looked at the ground and didn't respond. My mum immediately picked up on it and asked what was wrong. I told her Will had spent the whole day bragging about his mother's new car and how she'd be picking him up in it later. Now came the lesson. Mum told me I should have waved back, smiled, looked completely unaffected and happy for him and his mother's new purchase. I didn't get it. She told me that depriving him of the satisfaction of making me jealous would have made his entire day's showing off a waste, resulting in resentment. A waste of William's time and a huge win for me. I loved it. I absolutely loved it.

Depriving people of their desired reaction became my hobby. I was really put through my paces in secondary school when a friend of mine seemed to take sadistic delight in serpenting me with the desire of making me worry about things. Whether it was fake homework she said was due, or tests she said were that day, my remaining unresponsive, unflapped and altogether unaffected frustrated her no end. She'd try every angle to passive-aggressively argue with me. It's like she just wanted my attention any way she could get it. Her venomous blows struck me from every angle. Some people take delight in abusing the ways of my people to cause harm and distress. This is insulting to my heritage: we use our powers when we must, like getting to the bottom of a diary confession, not simply to inflict harm because we can. With great power comes great responsibility, and serpenting should only ever be used when absolutely necessary, and never without provocation.

This has been difficult for me to stick to, even in my romantic relationships. My ex-partner was so unbelievably manipulative that serpenting was the only way we communicated. All of her compliments were propelled by a shady backwards intention, something put in place to knock my confidence rather than to build it up. I'd become so used to reading between the lines that when I met Rosie I wasn't sure what were games and what was real. What's so refreshing about Rosie is that what you see really is what you get. She's so honest about how she feels, and if she ever thinks I'm serpenting she'll say, 'OK, what's going on here? Let's just have an honest conversation, no walls,' and then I resentfully back down to a place of vulnerability. I hate that place.

The Worst Types of People

Here's a generic and offensive list of some of the worst types of people:

■ People with weak handshakes. At what point in life did we forget the importance of a good handshake? There is nothing I hate more than a flaccid wrist and a distinct lack of grip when I'm meeting someone new. This can only be an indication of their slippery, non-committal nature.

■ Anyone who calls themself an 'entrepreneur' when actually they're just self-employed.

■ People who take photographs of themselves as if they aren't aware of the camera. WTF? You took the picture.

■ People who take pictures of themselves pretending to be asleep. You're not asleep, YOU TOOK THE PICTURE.

■ People who stop the 'cheers!' for the 'champagne shot'. The occasion is champagne, just let me drink it.

■ People who live to be constantly outraged. Get over your perpetual state of offence.

The Best Types of People

■ People eager to throw you an emergency laugh.

■ People who don't make judgements.

■ People who carry a spork.

■ People who remember the things that are important to you.

■ People who tell you if there's a small tree stuck in your teeth.

■ People willing to indulge in your dreams.

■ People willing to practise kissing *Cruel Intentions* style.

Let me tell you something about manners. They cost nothing but they're worth a lot. That was one saying that was drilled into us at primary school. That, and don't wipe your nose with your sleeve. Rosie obviously went to a different school. There's nothing I detest more than an arrogant, conceited twat who deems their self-worth so highly they don't consider manners to be important.

I hate seeing how success, fame and money can change people. Being grounded, staying in touch with your audience and not being divorced from reality are, the most important things any 'star' can do, and in my opinion, they're the key components of a long and successful career. As soon as you start believing you're better than your viewers, your friends, or even your family, you've lost it. You've become an entitled arse oozing cringe from every enlarged orifice. You ooze a similar brand of embarrassment as child stars who think they've hit the big time, but at least they don't know any better.

It's even worse when it's YouTubers. YouTube is a platform allowing anybody to upload their original content. If you're fortunate enough to become popular, your audience is absolutely everything. Unlike other careers in the entertainment industry, being a YouTuber is all about the relationship you have with the people watching your videos. You're backed solely by them, and every opportunity that comes to you is because they have put you on the map. To ever assume you've reached a point when you can forget your fans or take them for granted is the point when you've lost touch. Losing touch makes you completely unrelatable, unlikeable and no longer accessible. And being inaccessible to your audience means there's a distinction between you and them, which isn't what YouTube is about for me. I understand that for YouTubers with subscribers in the millions that the dynamic might change. You might not be able to walk out as easily in public, and you have to be smart about how much personal information you're willing to share for your own safety. But if you start to believe that you're popular because you're better, that your time is more precious because you're a 'business mogul' and not one of us, that you can start refusing people selfies because they don't directly contribute to your channel growth, then what are you really in it for?

I don't consider myself famous, but YouTube stars constitute a new brand of celebrity which isn't fully understood yet by mainstream media. And as much as I sit here and criticise those who have seemingly lost touch, I have experienced what it's like when subscribers overstep boundaries, which I'm sure is only magnified when your subscribers are in the multi-millions. That's one of the difficulties in maintaining a strong relationship with your viewers without sacrificing your own privacy. Fortunately the majority of our online fans are incredibly respectful, not only to us but to each other, and we're very lucky to have garnered the considerate audience that we have. I've only ever met a handful who have tried to steal my hair for a potion, and even then I respected their commitment. No matter who you are, what you do or what circles you move in, remaining courteous, respectful and grounded will strengthen every relationship that you have and will encourage the right ones.

ROSIE

Why don't we set some social media ground rules, seeing as we are all guilty of the same online faux pas? Next time social media EVER makes you feel less than, you can recap on these rules and chill.

SOCIAL MEDIA GROUND RULES

■ Stop comparing yourself to people on Instagram/social media in general. We all know the same tricks – we all do them. Social media is full of people posing awkwardly to make their bodies appear more toned and slender, airbrushing wrinkles, spots, scars and marks, people with thick make-up on who look EXACTLY the same as you or me when they are make-up-free. I'm sat here writing this book with about twenty layers of prescription moisturiser on my winter-chapped skin. I look greasy. I can feel a large boil forming on my right cheek. My hair is scraped back and I'm wearing joggers. I don't know HOW some people look AMAZING in joggers on Insta while I always look like a boiled egg drowning in dog-haired fabric. There are gaps in my eyebrows. My cave smells like old tea. But THAT'S OK. It's OK for these people to want to look obnoxiously attractive on Instagram and it's OK that nobody looks like that 24/7. You are no less than these people. Everybody is worth the same. Everybody is trying their best. Everybody feels and looks like shit some of the time. That's OK. You can stop comparing.

■ Stop bragging, and stop checking up on people and wondering if they've seen your latest post. It doesn't matter how well anyone else is doing. The only person you should compete with is your former self. That way you can constantly improve and become a better person. Everybody is in a different life situation, so comparison is futile.

■ Remember that people probably aren't having as much fun as you think they are, OR if they are, that's OK too! Don't feel down if someone seems to have more money, more trips to exotic places, more friends or more likes. Everybody in the world goes through ups and downs. Your life will get better, and these people will go through some lows and some more highs.

■ Be kind, always! Everyone is fighting an invisible battle no one else knows about. Be careful with your words. Think before you tweet. And finally . . .

■ Be positive whenever possible! This is probably the best rule ever. Positivity is contagious. I think we can all agree that you'd much rather scroll through your timeline and see something positive than some horrendous piece of news or soul-destroying story. I don't want to unexpectedly read something that brings down my mood for the rest of the day. It's not physically possible to be spreading happiness 24/7, but if you spread the love as much as possible, I don't see how that could ever be a bad thing!

Talking about comparing yourself to the goddesses of Instagram brings us to FOMO. Fear Of Missing Out. I suffer from this occasionally, as I can't stand the thought of other people having a better time than me.

It's typical human nature to want what we can't have, which is why everyone else's Nando's always looks better than yours. *Ahh, why didn't I order that?* you sigh inwardly. It's exactly the same in social situations. When you're at home with your feet up and crumbs around your mouth you may regret not accepting the invitation to that thing. Worse still, you may lament the complete lack of invitation at all. But I bet you've all been on a night out and let your eyes glaze over imagining all the things you'll do when you get home. Take off your binding clothes. Eat that leftover pasta. Put the heating on and watch *Gilmore Girls*, waiting for Rory and Lorelai to *finally* kiss. The list of fun stuff you can do at home suddenly becomes endless when you're not there.

In fact, Rose has taken the time to diligently make a list of things that are ALL worth staying in for:

A packet of jelly beans.

Mixing two types of cereal.

Purposely sending voice notes to the wrong friends pretending you're bitching about them, LOL.

Seeing if a radiator toasts a marshmallow.

Thanks for that, Rose.

Social Anxiety

We can't discuss our social lives, or lack thereof, without mentioning social anxiety. For me this was something that didn't exist in my world, until one day it arrived, bringing along with it a suitcase, a toothbrush and a stubborn refusal to leave.

Social anxiety affects me even at the mere *thought* of being social, which is a paradox because I like to think of myself as a confident and friendly, outgoing person. I like people, I LOVE hearing about people's lives, their jobs, what they get up to. I also like talking to people. But I worry. I worry *so much*.

I worry that what I just said wasn't funny. I worry that everyone thinks I'm weird. I worry that everyone secretly hates me or at the very least finds me annoying. I worry that my outfit is wrong for the occasion, that I stand out. I worry that people have noticed my insecurities and are judging me for them. In fact, here's a list of things I worry about on a regular basis:

■ People silently judging the way I eat.

■ That there is something on my face or in my teeth that shouldn't be there.

■ Seeing someone clock a spot on my face and watching their eyes flit between the spot and my gaze.

■ Breaking wind in an enclosed area, for example, in a car or in a room with just one other person.

■ Everyone falling silent, and the mental frenzy that comes with finding something to talk about.

■ Ass paranoia. This wasn't always something I worried about, until an incident when I arrived at the train station ready for a night out while unknowingly flapping around a metre of loo roll that was protruding from my bottom.

So how do you overcome social anxiety when you desperately want to be social, or at the very least want to feel comfortable and at ease? Well, I've written a few tips that might help you. For starters, remember that everyone has felt awkward, shy and anxious at some point, so you aren't alone. People have been through this before and got through it! You can do this!

> **Prepare.** I know myself and my body extremely well and I have been pretty public when it comes to discussing my bodily habits. When I'm anxious I know that I will inevitably be rushing to the bathroom. Before I do live events, radio shows or anything that I feel is important or where people will be listening closely, I get diarrhoea. (This book isn't called *Overshare* for no reason!) For events that aren't quite as important but still get my adrenaline pumping, my body responds by forcing me to empty my bladder multiple times. Knowing this is how I react helps me prepare. I always carry Imodium in my bag and I go to the loo as much as possible, and I occasionally limit my water

intake! If you know your body reacts to stressful situations by having stomachs cramps, bring painkillers. If you stress-sweat, carry a small stick of deodorant and wear loose clothes. If you prepare for the worst it can reassure you that you'll cope in any anxiety-inducing situation.

Try to get out of your own head. We are all guilty of over-thinking. But there comes a point when you have to stop fretting over every possible eventuality and just go for it. Which leads me to my next point . . .

Face your fear. I've done this countless times and let me tell you, it is so rewarding! If you thought I wasn't afraid of standing onstage in front of thousands of people you were wrong. On stage I have felt totally naked. There is nowhere to hide. But the feeling that hits me when I finish a show is overwhelmingly positive. If you push yourself to go to something you are worried about and end up having a fantastic time, it will make you more inclined to go again next time. Give it a chance!

People are kinder than you think. You worry that all eyes are on you, judging you. But are you judging other people? Picking them apart, internally criticising them? I know I'm not; I try my hardest to smile at people and make friends. Chances are, the people you are surrounded by might have the exact same worries and nerves that you have. They might be feeling even worse! Give people a chance – you never know where it might lead.

And finally, smile! Sometimes you just have to fake it till you make it. Wear a big smile and you will look approachable. Also, it's hard to feel too bad when you are smiling. Take a deep breath, hold your head up, smile, and give them all you've got! Sometimes doing our best is the best we can do.

ROSE

Over the last few years, Rosie and I have met a lot of people from different industries, and we've made some excellent friends. We like to be close to the people we work with because gelling as a unit makes life so much easier, especially if we're touring the world. We make sure to surround ourselves with the best team so that whatever we're working on results in the best possible outcome. Having creative goals in common and feeling excited about the content we're creating is something that has brought us together with people who are now some of our closest friends and colleagues! It proves that even as we grow older, new people will come into our lives, and that there's always space for new friendships. So give people a chance, but know your limits, and never expect perfection. No one is perfect, so don't let what could be a potentially amazing friendship slip away! Don't give up on people. Not everyone is shit, only the majority!

Sometimes you WILL have to walk away from people, and uncomfortable situations like that keep Rosie awake at night. Well, not really, that girl sleeps like a narcoleptic sperm whale, but it definitely makes her anxious. But I've come to realise that friends come and go and that life is like a bus journey. As you're driving along, some people will get on and some will get off. Some will stick with you until your final destination, and others will skedaddle at the end of the mixtape. Some people might get off only to get on again a few stops later! You might even find yourself throwing people off the bus, and underneath it, and that's OK! Just don't drop below 50mph, because you never know if Dennis Hopper has alternative plans for you.

ROSIE

Boundaries are something I'm still trying to figure out, although Rose and I have had a safe word since the very beginning of our relationship. It's important to know where to draw the line with some people. Following suit of Dua Lipa, I've written down some rules, or guidelines really, that you might find helpful when it comes to knowing your own limits.

It's OK to want space from people. No one should make you feel guilty for needing some time alone, or away. I've learned that the best friends are the ones you can pick up the phone and call and nothing has changed, no matter how many weeks, months or years have flown by.

It's OK not to have friends for a while. If the friends you do have are making you feel drained and lacking in confidence, you should feel fine about letting go and giving yourself some time on your own. I think it's brave to make the decision to have no friends rather than the wrong ones. You need to surround yourself with positive people!

Everyone gets dropped. It's not you. (Well, it might be, but that's not very uplifting!) Listen, we've all been unexpectedly dropped by friends at some point, and it's easy to take it personally. But as long as you try your hardest to treat people with kindness, sometimes you've just got to accept that not everything works out. Maybe you made a mistake that you can learn from, but maybe it just wasn't meant to be. You can't always get closure after a relationship ends, so . . .

Move on. Don't ruminate, let it go! When you stop holding on to the past you make room for the future and for amazing new people to enter your life!

No friend is perfect. So don't expect them to be. They will annoy you at times and you will annoy them. A friendship is compromise, so accept people's flaws.

Be yourself. If you like something, talk about it. No one else in the world can be you. Everybody is unique, so celebrate yourself!

CHAPTER 6
GIRL POWER

'You are stronger than you think you are, always.'

ROSIE

Girl power. Something I learned about extensively from the Spice Girls, and something I am truly passionate about. I hate injustice, I hate sexism, but more than anything, I hate that Geri left.

I never used to be that into politics, but there have always been causes I've been passionate about. Many years of watching Disney's *Pocahontas* has conditioned me into having a deep and profound respect for the environment, and if something that could have been recycled gets put into the wrong bin, I feel tremendously guilty. Naturally, marrying a woman, being bisexual, and garnering a predominantly LGBT audience has flung me even deeper into politics than I could have ever imagined. We don't live in a world where all the rules are the same, and we don't live in a world where everyone is treated equally. As well as wanting equal treatment for the LGBTQ+ community, I want equal treatment for people of all races, ethnicities and genders. I wish for the equality of all humans.

Like everyone, I get upset about the injustices in the world. Sometimes it can get on top of you. You can think, *I am just one person. How can one person fight such powerful forces?* It's easy to feel overwhelmed. But each day I'm reminded that Rose and I have a platform and an audience, and we have a voice.

I've already discussed how Rose and I began our journey feeling under-qualified to speak out on behalf of the LGBTQ+ community, but we slowly found our voices when we saw that we could make a difference. Suddenly we realised that it wasn't just about the LGBTQ+ community anymore, but about everyone. We could help people by speaking about Rose's OCD, by discussing anxiety, relationships, or even simply by listening to our audience and letting them choose topics for us to discuss.

Change can start in small ways, and instead of feeling like perhaps I wasn't qualified to discuss these topics, I realised that actually it was my born right, regardless of our YouTube platform. I'm a person who lives on this earth too! My experiences and my feelings count. I'm allowed to speak up and say my piece.

I hoped I could help educate people online, but at the same time, I was also learning a lot. Although global politics is arguably more turbulent now than ever before, I couldn't help but notice the incredibly powerful movements that are happening. For example, the Black Lives Matter marches and hashtag on Twitter. Growing up in an extremely small town, I'd never been awakened to just how oppressed some people are in the world. But through the power of the internet, and ordinary people sharing posts on Facebook and retweeting videos on Twitter, messages get spread and, more importantly, messages get heard. I can remember seeing an extremely shocking video about a nurse who refused to give a patient's blood work to a police officer who did not possess the required warrant. This woman was verbally abused by the officer and was later arrested. Watching the video left me seething at the injustice. But because it was filmed, uploaded and spread via the internet, it could no longer be ignored, and the police officer in question lost his job. Justice was served.

Another powerful message being spread via the internet is the #MeToo movement. The movement was actually started in 2006 by Tarana Burke, and originated when she listened to a young girl's story of abuse. At the time, Tarana wanted to tell the girl, 'Me too,' but couldn't. But the idea was born. #MeToo has since become a viral, rallying cry and an attempt to demonstrate the magnitude of people, both men and women, who have suffered from rape and sexual abuse. I have personally seen waves being made, have witnessed – almost solely through the power of the internet – people becoming more aware and more educated on subjects such as equality, victim-blaming, slut-shaming, cultural appropriation, racism, feminism and many more powerful subjects that need discussing.

My eyes were being opened. I used to be someone who didn't vote. I didn't understand politics, I thought it was simply too great a subject for me to tackle, but I registered, I researched and I voted, and I encouraged others to do the same. Perhaps controversially, I honestly didn't care who other people voted for, I just wanted them to vote. I have learned to respect everybody's opinions, even if they don't align with my own. I've found that kindness and compassion is the best way to reach someone, although I'll admit, it took me a while to learn that.

As you start to dip your toes, or even wade, into the thick, messy waters of politics, it can be easy to get swept away. The more I understood, the less I could accept that that's how things were. Gun control, the mistreatment of innocent animals, the imbalance of the justice system, the fear mongering of the tabloids, racism, prejudice. I became overwhelmed, and had to take a step back for a while. I wanted to be an activist, to help people, but for my own sanity I realised that sometimes it's OK to take a break from these things.

But that's the thing with change. The world keeps turning, things keep happening, and you have to stay positive! You have to fight, and most importantly, you have to keep going!

So let's get on to the issues that need tackling, starting with sexism.

ROSE

I hate sexism. I hate it more than other people's spit landing on my lip and having to pretend like I didn't notice. I'm confident when I say most women have experienced sexism at some point in their lives. Coming from men it doesn't much surprise me – though obviously it's uneducated and beyond moronic – but when it comes from women, THAT I can't fathom.

When I used to advise people on Apple hardware back in my days of retail, there were countless times I'd be overlooked as customers beelined for my male colleagues. Older men were the worst offenders, but several older women spurned my offer to help because they assumed I didn't know as much as the male staff. Technology? Women? How could those two things possibly go together? My tiny female mind could never have the intellectual capacity of a man's! I could never be expected to retain knowledge like a man could, nor could I truly understand the information I *had* managed to cram into my hopelessly underdeveloped girl-brain. Ridiculous. Nope, they'd rather save their time and talk to someone reliable with a penis credential.

Due to the nature of my job, gender-stereotyping was something I constantly had to battle, and most days I enjoyed the challenge. While working at the store, I distinctly remember approaching an elderly female customer to ask if she needed any assistance. Now, this lady wasn't frail – she was in sound mind, and one would HATE to assume considering the topic we're discussing – but I imagined she only needed her iPad for Candy Crush Jelly Saga and games to enhance her memory. BUT HEY, she might have been writing a novel, dialling in to video conferences or hacking security systems! Just because she was older didn't mean she was useless. That's ageism and is something I'm sure I'll experience once I'm thirty.

As the words 'Is there anything I can help you with?' passed my lips, the lady looked at me, visibly humoured by my offer, drew the cover over her iPad screen and said, 'I think it's best I speak to one of those men.' I replied with, 'Well, what's the issue? Perhaps it's something I can help with.' I was concerned she'd notice the blood dripping onto my T-shirt from where I'd bitten through my tongue, but I needn't have worried, she was already gone. Ironically, she'd approached the most inept member of staff in the history of retail and human development, so I thought that was punishment enough for her sexist thinking. With a mentality like that I wanted to ask her why she assumed her woman-shaped mind would be able to grasp my male colleague's explanation. I mean, if I wasn't able to grasp technology as a woman, why would she?

Defying people's crude assumptions by having the knowledge they needed to overcome their technical issues was extremely rewarding, delicious even! But it wasn't just the customers I had to contend with. Even my bosses treated me differently when push came to shove.

I worked with three men. There were four full-timers, myself included, and our job was to sell Apple hardware and teach customers how to use it. The boys never wanted to do the one-to-one tutorials because it required patience and, frankly, they couldn't be bothered. The shop was quiet most days, and between drinking coffee and the routine sexism, I'd often find myself enveloped in bubblewrap, seeing how long I could stand on one leg before falling over. But one thing was for sure: when it was time to work, I was there and I was present. I took huge satisfaction in being the best, selling the most, and being helpful, friendly and competent. It was the first job I'd had since graduating university, and it was one that I took pride in. I knew my abilities and my strengths and I knew when to ask for help if I needed it. I soon became the face of the YourTime sessions (as they were known), and always craved more responsibility. And yet at a staff meeting one morning, I experienced behaviour that was so shocking it led to my decision to walk out.

A friend of the store owner had popped into the shop and relayed information about his customer experience. His feed-back included members of staff failing to approach customers and instead standing idle on their phones on the shop floor. Well, I knew that wasn't me. The bubblewrap restricted arm movement, so I certainly wouldn't have been able to hold a phone. In all seriousness, I was always first to greet a customer and offer my help. Our manager had clearly got a bollocking from his offsite superior and had decided it was time to point fingers. In our staff meeting he was visibly angry about the feedback. But instead of talking to us as a team he found it far easier to focus his eyes on me. He was extremely pally with his male co-workers as he'd worked alongside them for years before I'd joined the company. It was clear that he felt uncomfortable reprimanding them so decided to centre his attention exclusively on me. 'We can't just play on our phones all day and ignore customers! It's not good enough! I'm sick of people standing behind the computer all day browsing the internet! Customers are our top priority!

I agreed with everything he was saying. But why was he only looking at me? I didn't take cigarette breaks, I didn't avoid engaging with customers, but I was being made to accept full responsibility because I was an easy target. I was the youngest, I was a woman, and I wasn't his mate. His unmerited targeting became so obvious that I felt embarrassed on his behalf and my colleagues were noticeably uncomfortable. He was too cowardly to speak to us about it collectively in case he damaged the relationship he had with his friends, and I was forced to take accountability for everyone because I was a woman. No doubt about it. Well, I wasn't going to accept that. 'Why are you only looking at me?' I asked. I hadn't been singled out by the secret shopper, so what evidence was there that I was exclusively at fault? I was so confident in my performance that I doubted the blame lay with me. My boss didn't have a lot to say when I questioned his conduct. I'd had enough. I grabbed my jacket, nailed my 'pissed-off with purpose' exit walk, and left. It was the most pathetic male performance I'd ever witnessed, and as I walked through town I realised that I'd sacrificed my job for the greater good of womankind. I felt accomplished. I felt independent. I felt financially vulnerable. I MEAN BRAVE.

ROSIE

Now, you might think we're coming across as brash and whiny, and trust me I get it. Rose can be particularly shrill when she's upset, like most women get when they're hysterical. LOL. And I understand that there are bigger problems in the world, and that there are still people who are starving, who are homeless, who are sick and can't afford healthcare. I know we should be strong and we shouldn't sweat the small stuff. But for me, being strong means not standing for even the smallest amount of gender stereotyping, and never allowing a man to talk down to me because he is older or simply because he's a man.

Let's talk about Julia Roberts in *Pretty Woman* a moment. Several years ago, Rose and I opened our first merch store, which we completely ran and organised ourselves. Before the store went live we looked into options of how best to deliver merchandise to our customers around the world. We had a pretty accurate projection of how much we would sell and our focus was how to get our products out as quickly as possible to everyone who had ordered them.

Luckily, there was a global courier service just a few doors down from where we were living! Problem solved. So Rose and I popped in, approached the man working there and enquired about prices, postage, the works.

This guy did NOT want us to use his postal service. He repeatedly talked down to us, saying we had to have 'lots of orders' to qualify for this service. After questioning how many orders we'd need to qualify, we received a hesitant and seemingly speculative answer of a hundred orders. 'That's fine!' we said, and then he endeavoured to find out whether we were selling make-up, make-up brushes or old clothes we wanted to get rid of. We told him we were running a clothing store, and he resentfully mumbled something about fashion. This man wasn't going to move an inch. He offered every excuse in the book not to serve us, as he didn't believe we'd be successful enough to waste his time on.

So, being the grudge holders that we are and totally unwilling to let anything go, we opened our merch store (using a different courier service), and later went back to pay the man a visit. We told him we'd opened the store, and he grinned and said, 'Did you get many orders?' 'Yes,' we replied. 'We got 2,200 orders in our first week and we're here to by some printer ink for our order forms.' He then had the AUDACITY to backtrack in an attempt to claw back our custom. NEVER. He didn't believe we'd do well. He didn't believe we knew what we were talking about. He thought we were overestimating our sales predictions and that there'd be little demand for our 'make-up brushes'. He assumed we were selling make-up because we were women. But even if we were, what difference does that make in terms of our need for his service? I have no time for people who don't believe women can be successful just because they are women.

ROSE

Rosie, you're getting really worked up – maybe it's your period.

It's bizarre how some men decide to have arguments with women just because they're women. I've been in countless situations when I've been spoken to like I was lesser, like I was stupid, or have been belittled by someone abusing their position of power. I walk away thinking, *There's no way he would have engaged in a confrontation like that if I'd been a man.* I distinctly remember losing my train ticket once, leaving me with nothing to present at the barrier of my destination. As annoying as it was, I was fully willing to pay whatever fee I'd incurred by travelling without a ticket. When Rosie and I approached the man working at the station, I began to explain my dilemma. He didn't even pretend to listen to me. Before I could even finish my sentence he said it was an offence to travel without a valid ticket. If he'd let me finish, he'd have understood that I agreed with him and was willing to pay the fine. But of course, he DIDN'T let me finish, he barely let me begin.

Before I could even ask how much I owed he said, 'THAT'S AN IMMEDIATE FINE FOR TRAVELLING WITHOUT A TICKET.' As I was asking how much that would be, he yelled, 'HELLOOOOOOOOOOOOO?!' I was mid-sentence. What was happening here? He accused me of speaking 'at' him. He'd just interrupted ME, but there was something about the conversation he'd misinterpreted or was unable to follow. He was getting very hot under the collar and increasingly aggressive. He wanted an argument. I softly replied saying that I wasn't speaking 'at' him, only 'to' him, as that's what's necessary to have a conversation between two people. I said he was incredibly rude but I was more than willing to pay the on-the-spot fine and asked him again to kindly tell me how much it was.

Well, he wasn't expecting THAT and he looked almost disappointed at how agreeable I was being. Instead, he puffed up his chest, realised he was on to a losing battle of composure and politeness, walked *slowly* over to the barrier and opened the gate with his keys. 'You're lucky this time.' Lucky? I'd just been publicly shouted at for offering to pay the penalty! This was a classic example of a man abusing his power. Was I supposed to be grateful for his kind act of generosity? Get fucked. I'd have preferred to go through the time-consuming process of paying the fine just so that he'd have a laborious task to undertake so he could take a break from being a twat. Some people might argue that he'd have behaved exactly the same way towards a man in my situation, but I don't believe it. When it comes to men asserting their power over woman, I have experienced quite an array.

Rosie, do you remember the time you repeatedly hit that man's car window, called him a twat and completely LOST YOUR SHIT?

ROSIE

Yes. But we had pedestrian right of way and he aggressively beeped at us to move so he could leave his parking space! We weren't even in the middle of a road!

ROSE

I'm just pleased that you've grown as a person and can turn the other cheek. I'm also pleased that you scared him SO much he sped away in a panic because he didn't expect to anger such a turbulent beast.

But sexism occurs in the most unlikely of places and in some extremely commonplace ones. Even my grandad used to ask if I was being looked after by a man, like I was weak, defenceless and in need of saving. Of course, he meant no harm, but he'd ask so frequently that I'd feel obliged to put his mind at rest, so I developed the character of Hoytt. Hoytt was my fictitious Scandinavian love interest, a tree surgeon by day and an on-call veterinarian by night. He was the quintessence of heteronormative masculinity, and in years to come would become an integral character in our *Exposed* tour! But before I can be accused of not educating my grandad on women's strength and self-reliance, one has to bear in mind the generation of his upbringing, plus I forgave him on account of his good intentions. My point here is that the idea of women being weak was so ingrained into society that even his love and care were spurred by sexist abstraction.

This generational clash brought with it gender stereotypes that needed to be broken down and forgotten. Not dissimilar to Grandma's 'ice square' (a hard dessert best eaten on the day).

ROSIE

What I'm beginning to understand is that most of us, unconsciously, have internal judgements that are a result of the society we have been raised in. I'm not even that old, but when I was in school girls weren't allowed to play football and boys didn't do dance! These 'rules' that we are fed get subconsciously ingrained into our mindsets, and we have to work extremely hard to question why we think a certain way. I try really hard to consider why I feel the way I do before I make a judgement.

I do see a change in society for the better. Gone are the days when women were inclined to say 'I'm not like other girls' in an attempt to set themselves apart from the stereotypes that were forced onto the generic label of 'girl'. Now women rally together in women's protests and marches. Women can proudly say they *are* like other women. That doesn't mean that all females love make-up or the colour pink. It means that it doesn't matter whether they wear no make-up at all or colour themselves in glitter. It doesn't matter if women wear suits, play video games, have short hair, or don't subscribe to a particular gender norm.

I'm convinced that the only way forward is to support each other. In a society of outrage culture, rather than coming at people with an immediately reactive response, it's great to look at a situation from all angles.

ROSE

Rosie, wait! I haven't finished moaning about my silly women problems intensified by my hormones! So, before we discuss how to overcome sexism I have one more story that involves sexism from YouTube itself! This is a particularly juicy one guaranteed to leave you woke . . .

Last year Rosie and I were put forward for a YouTube grant, which would allow us to finance a creative project that we would pitch to a select board of members. We'd done extremely well even to have been put forward, and we thought it was the perfect opportunity to give the LGBTQ+ community even more mainstream exposure.

We were asked what our plans for the future were, to which

we responded, 'Remaining entertaining, remaining visible, expanding our family and being visibly representative of our community.' The male staff member didn't seem particularly interested during our interview. Fine. Perhaps these were areas he felt didn't warrant financial investment. That was his prerogative and I respected his opinion. Until, that is, he began to question our ability to be parents and simultaneously have a career on YouTube.

'And you think you could manage having a baby and doing YouTube? Have you thought about how tiring and difficult that might be? Having a baby and vlogging might be hard to juggle.'

What was he asking us? If we'd be able to manage a full-time job and have children? Like we hadn't considered what it meant to be working parents, or that because we were female, we wouldn't be able to cope? Would he ask the same question a man? I couldn't believe what I was hearing from a guy in his late twenties. What was even more uncomfortable was that his female superior was also on the Skype call looking awkward as FUCK, but remained silent, waiting for us to answer his moronic question.

'If you're asking whether the two of us believe we will cope with a child AND a career, the answer is yes. We have considered that.'

HOW INSULTING. I knew we'd be unsuccessful with the grant but I wasn't going to let that one slide. What bothers me the most is people assuming I'm playing the sexist card. Well, I have a trillion cards I could play, and sexism is just one of them. But just because I have them at my disposal doesn't mean I'm drawing them without justification. It's very easy to shut someone down with the accusation that they're using prejudice as their pretext. But no matter how understanding, sensitive and fair men can be, they will never experience what it's like to be discriminated against as a woman.

ROSIE

If there's one thing I've learned, it's that we can't just sit here and moan about our problems all day. We have to get up and make change happen, starting with ourselves. As much as I like to feel that I am 'woke' and 'progressive', I'm self-aware enough to realise that I still have a long way to go. I'm problematic, we all are.

We've all made mistakes. It's OK to admit that – after all, how can you change if you think you are already perfect? The world is constantly evolving and it's easy to slip up, especially if you didn't realise you were doing something wrong. For instance, remember the online catchphrase of saying something was your 'spirit animal'? I've since come to learn that this is a form of cultural appropriation of indigenous peoples and their culture.

Thankfully, society is progressing and I am seeing a surge in political correctness and generally more awareness of other people. More awareness of disabilities, ethnicities, the treatment of minorities, and I'm noticing how many people on the internet are spreading these positive messages. I honestly can't convey how much I've learned from the internet, and I still continue to learn!

But I've seen the downsides too. There's a Tumblr account called Your Fave Is Problematic, dedicated to highlighting any slight wrongdoing of those in the public eye. I find this particularly unfair. Everybody makes mistakes, but not everyone has to make them in public, and having your face rubbed in it is even worse. I've seen YouTubers trending over old tweets and these witch hunts aren't always helpful. How would you feel if you got caught out being a massive dumbass and an angry mob brought their pitchforks and burned you at the stake for it? As of yet, no one has invented a time machine to go back and correct past ignorance. But usually that's exactly what it is – ignorance, rather than hatred. The important thing is that you can change who you are and how you act today, and this is something I am working on every second. Allow yourselves to evolve. We're only human after all, and we're all guilty of making mistakes!

I'm learning that if you want to better the world, start with yourself and set an example. I've also learned that positivity is contagious and that it's ridiculously difficult to bitch with a person who's just not joining in. I've given up bad habits and I've taken up a hell of a lot of good ones! I try to challenge and question myself every day and spread love as much as possible. I may not be able to give everyone in the world money but I can definitely pay people a compliment. I love saying really loudly, 'Oh my God, I LOVE that girl's outfit!' as people walk by me. I love smiling at strangers, I love tweeting positive vibes. I've cut out a lot of hate-fuelling websites, and I'm sorry but I've had to unfollow or at least mute anyone who's consistently negative. I try to spread love and I try to be as educated as I can be. But, guys, all I can do is try my best. But trust me, it's a great feeling knowing I'm doing all I can, and it's something I encourage you to do too.

I've recently come to learn a bit about intersectional feminism. The word 'intersectionality' was coined by American civil rights advocate and law professor Kimberlé Crenshaw in 1989. Crenshaw recognised that society often treated issues of race and gender as though they were mutually exclusive, when really that shouldn't be the case.

As we know, people are oppressed for a multitude of reasons, including gender, race, sexuality, class, ability and other variables that can impact our individual experiences of life. If an individual or individuals are a crossroad of these intersectional systems of society, they are likely to be victims of greater bias and oppression. For instance, I am a woman who is in a same-sex relationship, so I suffer from inequality due to my gender and due to my sexual orientation. However, in society I have benefited by being a cisgender person who is white and able-bodied. It's extremely important to realise that although feminism strives for equality for all people, we must recognise that some people are born with more privilege than others.

When discussing feminism it is important to bear in mind that what works for one person may not work for others, and that we should not only check our own privilege but also acknowledge the privilege (or lack thereof) in others.

A person who not only did this, but did it well is Emma Watson. She addressed her white privilege in a letter to her book club. She wrote:

> When I gave my UN speech in 2015, so much of what I said was about the idea that 'being a feminist is simple!' Easy! No problem! I have since learned that being a feminist is more than a single choice or decision. It's an interrogation of self . . . When I heard myself being called a 'white feminist' I didn't understand (I suppose I proved their case in point). What was the need to define me — or anyone else for that matter — as a feminist by race? What did this mean? Was I being called racist? Was the feminist movement more fractured than I had understood? I began . . . panicking.

> It would have been more useful to spend the time asking myself questions like: What are the ways I have benefited from being white? In what ways do I support and uphold a system that is structurally racist? How do my race, class and gender affect my perspective? There seemed to be many types of feminists and feminism. But instead of seeing these differences as divisive, I could have asked whether defining them was actually empowering and bringing about better understanding. But I didn't know to ask these questions.

I recently read up on the way the internet is designed, specifically social media. Using similar techniques to gambling websites, social platforms want you to spend as long as possible browsing, and will do everything in their power to stop you from clicking off onto another site, or, God forbid, turning off your device.

A 2013 study, from Beihang University in Beijing, of a Twitter-like site called Weibo, found that anger was the emotion that spread the most quickly over social media. Although joy came in second, it was analysed that outrage was rewarded with far more traction, as people preferred to share joy with intimate friends and peers, whereas with outrage, people were more likely to join in with strangers. When it comes to outrage, people are seeking validation for their opinions, be that through likes and comments or shares and retweets. There are also multiple studies on people's addiction to social media, as receiving a comment or a like gives a rush of dopamine, similarly to what happens when you smoke a cigarette or drink alcohol. Now, I am in no way hating on the very platform that gave me my career. I love the internet, I love that you can make friends, interact with people, make videos, share stories, share jokes, and just generally enjoy all the positives that come with staying connected. But nothing in the world is without its downsides, and I do believe that the negatives of social media need to be addressed. If outrage and quick reactive assumptions are being passed on from one stranger to another, I don't think that's altogether progressive. I believe there are times when we need to breathe, step away and recentre ourselves. It can be so easy to get swept away by fearmongering, sensationalist headlines, or to become upset by something before you've heard the full story.

It's time to stop tearing each other apart and start building each other up. And this is what I have learned from an intersectional approach to feminism: that compassion, empathy and an under-standing for others is key. Before we jump to conclusions, let's remind each other that the world isn't actually that bad a place and that generally people are wonderful.

ROSE

Rosie, what a highly articulate argument! You must have heard it from a man. Well done for reiterating it so skilfully. And I'm in total agreement with you: Emma Watson's a babe. BUT THAT'S NOT ALL SHE IS AND SHOULD NEVER BE VALUED FOR HER PHYSICAL ATTRIBUTES ALONE. It's so important for women to support other women! We are powerful alone but together we're a force to be reckoned with! Like when ants come together and carry objects a zillion times their own weight. That's us women carrying men towards each and every one of their successes. JUST KIDDING! THAT'S A SEXIST GENERALISED STATEMENT, LOL!

Now, in fear of any of you ever feeling discriminated against as women, by men, I've made a quick guide on what not to stand for. Follow these rules and you can't go wrong! Remember, I'm an influencer. I know what I'm talking about.

How to Combat Everyday Sexism

■ Never let a man hold the door open for you. How DARE you assume I'm too physically pathetic to hold the weight of a door, you pig-ignorant bastard.

■ Never let a man compliment you. OH, YOU THINK I'M INSECURE AND NEED COMPLIMENTING TO SURVIVE MY DAY? You inconsiderate prick.

■ Never allow a man to let women and children go first. OH, SO YOU THINK BECAUSE I'M A WOMAN MY CHANCES OF SURVIVAL ARE LESS THAN YOURS? Let's see shall we?!

■ Don't ever let them get the bill. OH, YOU THINK I CAN'T AFFORD IT DO YOU? That's not chivalry, that's boasting about the gender pay gap. Don't stand for it!

■ Do NOT let them stand up for you. You do NOT need them to fight your battles.

■ Never allow a man to be honest with you. They assume you can't play games because you're incapable of handling manipulation. Not the case.

ROSIE

Of course, we are all guilty of certain misconceptions, judgements and stereotypes. We even hold ourselves up to impossible standards. How many of us want to be a certain weight or fit the mould of a certain classification of beauty? I had a female friend who turned to me once and told me that 'there are no funny female comedians' because 'woman can't be funny'. I was shocked, but the only person she was limiting was herself. That's what we do when we decide to live by the rules, and believe that we can only act, think or look a certain way. But no one ever made history by following the rules.

There are a lot of women out there who I see talking the talk but not actually walking the walk. Women who spout a load of spiel about supporting other women – but what are they actually doing themselves? Ladies, let's all try harder.

First things first: we have got to stop bitching about one another. Don't reduce another women (or person) to their looks alone. Society already plays women off against each other with 'who is sexier?' and 'who wore it better?' Newsflash, they both look great! Besides, we're more than just objects to be lusted over and we are smart enough to know this already.

Help each other out and talk about pay. A lot of the female YouTubers in my field discuss pay with one another, not to gloat or flaunt, but to check that we are being paid fairly and equally and are not being ripped off. We offer each other advice and introduce our friends to people who might be beneficial to their careers. Why? Because TEAMWORK makes the DREAM WORK, ladies. When another woman is successful we should celebrate it. The more successful women out there, the more opportunities we all get!

ROSE

I'm really proud of what Rosie and I have achieved as women. Don't get me wrong, we've slept our way to the top, but that doesn't mean we haven't had our hurdles. We've had a lot on our side, there's no denying it. We're far from the biggest success story on the internet, but two LGBT women trying to make it in comedy isn't as easy as it might look. Especially when only one of us is funny.

Funny or talented women in Hollywood who might not necessarily adhere to the rigid, somewhat archaic standards of 'Hollywood appeal' inspire me to believe that you can achieve whatever you want to achieve as long as you're passionate, you're talented and you're driven, regardless of your age, race, shape or gender. Kristen Wiig, Rebel Wilson, Whoopi Goldberg, Ellen Page, Jennifer Hudson and Kristen Stewart have all encouraged me to be motivated. Women are doing it. Women are making waves, rejecting norms and speaking out, and here's how a few of them are doing it . . .

ROSIE

Evan Rachel Wood has had a profound impact on me recently. From wearing suits on the red carpet in order to challenge gender stereotypes and show girls that they can wear whatever they like, to speaking in front of Congress about her rapes and sexual assault. She's a feminist, a bisexual and an incredible actress! I like the way she uses her platform and social media accounts to spread positive messages. She doesn't argue with people online but still firmly promotes feminism and speaks openly about overcoming her past trauma. I find her extremely down to earth, relatable and talented.

Reese Witherspoon has been a hero of mine since *Legally Blonde*. The character Elle Woods showed me that I could be smart, ballsy, interesting and be taken seriously while still being extremely feminine and obsessed with pink and sparkles. Since then, Reese has gone on to create her production company, Pacific Standard, with the aim of seeing 'different, dynamic women on film'. She said: 'I was talking to my girlfriends who are actresses, and we were like, "There's nothing out there, they're really not making anything for us." So I thought, *Well then, I'll start a company, self-funded, and I'll start developing roles for women*. I'm really proud.' I admire Reese for her do-it-yourself attitude and I think it's amazing how she noticed a gap in the market and set out to fill it herself. As well as Pacific Standard, she has also created Hello Sunshine, a digital media company 'dedicated to telling female-driven stories, across all platforms'. Reese spoke about how she felt a responsibility for all the women in the world to create more opportunities for women, and that is something I truly commend.

Serena Williams. As well as her obvious physical talent and dedication, I admire Serena's strong attitude. For every negative comment, there's a million good comments. I always say, 'Not everyone's going to like the way I look.' Everyone has different types. If we all liked the same thing, it would make the world a really boring place! What matters most is that I like myself.

Serena has been criticised about her physical appearance, with people even telling her she needs to pluck her eyebrows. She says of the comments, 'Too muscly and too masculine, and then a week later too racy and too sexy. So for me it was just really a big joke.' Serena has praised the power of looking and being different and says that 'Since I don't look like every other girl, it takes a while to be OK with that. To be different. But different is good.'

ROSE

With these powerful women in mind, I've decided to articulate some advice for men. I think it's extremely well balanced, neither combative nor quarrelsome, and will prove instrumental in dissolving sexism. The world is changing. I truly believe we're going to experience a far more equal society, and the fair wording of my open letter supports the idea that men and women are equals.

Advice for Men

by Rose Dix

Hi, men. I'm writing this letter in hopes that it may act as the catalyst that spurs your awakening. Now, before you assume I'm about to attack, try not to jump to conclusions and let your hormones cloud your judgement. I don't hate you. I'm told that one of you actually contributed to my creation. But it's important for you to understand acceptable behaviour and recognise irreverence.

Women are smart, bold, loving but firm. We're determined and astute, we're creative visionaries and leaders whose powers are limitless. Don't pity us, don't underestimate us; we're at no disadvantage. It's not the same for you. You're men. You're automatically taken less seriously.

Now, this letter contains *information* that's in your own interests, so try to retain as much of this as possible. If you need help translating the text into something slightly more rudimental, please locate your nearest female colleague.

Let me put your mind at rest. There will come a point when you'll have to choose whether you'd like a career or a family. You can't have both, you won't manage. But don't fear this decision just because you're running out of time. Don't allow yourself to be pestered by the women at work who ask when you plan on starting a family, automatically assuming that you are able to have one. Just because it's naturally your primary goal it doesn't mean you should feel any external pressure to announce your plans. It's what you've been working towards your whole life, and when it does happen, don't feel like a failure on the days when you break down. Your wives will pick up the pieces because they're better able to remain composed.

However, don't be concerned if you decide to pursue your career and defy the very reason you were put on this earth: to give life. There's every chance that you'll progress up the career ladder and will make it to managing director, since every year, companies are forced to award high-calibre positions to men, to balance the overwhelming number of women in top-tier management. You may be lucky enough to benefit from positive discrimination – this way, at least they won't be basing your promotion on your aptitude or job performance.

I appreciate that it must be hard not to let testosterone steer your decision-making. I'd hate to be subservient to my genetic make-up, but on the occasions where we catcall you, try to positively respond or you risk receiving a low fuckability rating. This is an age-old method of ranking and is one that should certainly govern the way you choose to present yourself. Remember, it's the opinions of your female cohorts that matter most, even if you didn't desire them in the first place.

There may even be times when women explain things to you, assuming that you didn't already know. We only do this because usually we're right, especially when it comes to technology. It's important to recognise your own limits, and by standardising you, we save time. Sweeping generalisations and gender-based stereotyping allow us to categorise men into specialisms we deem lesser, unimportant or silly, so as women, we remain feeling unthreatened. When we require counsel regarding such disciplines as beauty, make-up or fashion, please sit tight, because you're our first point of call.

Now chin up – it might never happen!

CHAPTER 7
THE FUTURE

'If you're asking whether I'll love my biological baby more than your biological baby, the answer is yes.'

ROSIE

My impending future feels both daunting and immensely promising. It's also constantly happening: I keep worrying about the future and then I wake up the next day and I'm in it. Life keeps occurring; I clean the bathrooms and they need to be re-cleaned, I clear out my inbox and the emails pile in again. The dog is in a constant cycle of being walked or getting ready for her next one and I wake up and Rose is still there.

Our immediate future is exhilarating, all-consuming and exhausting. Right now and for the foreseeable time being, we are in the process of buying and moving into our first house, writing a book, and working on another secret project, all while attempting to juggle our usual uploading schedule and retain just enough of a social life that our friends don't ditch us completely. Selfishly, everyone decided to be been born during what is now our busiest time, and there's nothing that makes me feel guiltier than declining a birthday party invite from your bestie.

But I'm certainly not complaining. You don't learn about the power of positivity and then just forget it all! All of the above is so exciting! The other day Rose and I chose our first item of furniture for our new home and I squealed with joy. I'm just so grateful to even be able to buy a house, especially in such a difficult climate. I'm in such a wonderful position: I enjoy my job, I love my wife, and tomorrow is the first day of the rest of our lives. So what's next for us?

ROSE

The future. It's not tangible, it's not stable, but it's imminent, it's unavoidable, and the only thing that's certain about it is the fact that it's coming. Are we slaves to it, or are we the creators of our own path? Thinking about the future is bittersweet. On the one hand, I'm excited to turn into my father with his loathing of new technology and an eagerness to quarrel. But on the other hand, the inevitability of collapsing onto my fall mat because no one responded to my bedside buzzer is dire to say the least. I'm acutely aware that the longer I live the less time I have left to disprove that $E=mc^2$, or at least use it as my stage name. The older I get the more I begin to question life's purpose and appreciate Reese Witherspoon's refusal to age by cloning herself to become immortal. Do I want to become a cartoon combo of facial paralysis and a rubber chicken beak, or do I want to age with a little decorum? Well. I want the beak and strictly one facial expression. Does that mean I've succumbed to superficial societal values, or do most people who oppose cosmetic anti-ageing simply fail to see the multi-functionality the beak has to offer? Function one: lay your lips on your desk and you're your very own paperweight. Function two: they're shock-absorbent in the event of an air collision and buoyant in any open water that may follow. But despite the beak's organisation/lifesaving potential, I'm yet to fully commit.

ROSIE

I once read an article that claimed your thirties were some of the best years of your life. The summary of this article was that, stereotypically, you tend to experience a lot in your twenties, which you eventually learn how to deal with, and so you end up in a much better situation in your thirties. The article listed points such as: you've developed your own sense of style by thirty; you've become more accepting of yourself; and you've learned how to deal with irritating people at work.

I agreed with a lot of the article. I've been through a lot – career-wise and in my personal life – that I've learned lessons from. I've adopted new skills and rules to help protect myself and to keep me calmer in the face of stress. I feel I am more accepting of myself. But the one thing I can't get on board with is ageing. I just refuse to do it.

I'm OK with the getting older part – that's inevitable. I enjoy a good birthday party, so I'm looking forward to the ones to come. But the physical ageing upsets me. I just want to preserve my face, and it can't be impossible because Nicole Kidman has done it.

I don't want anything invasive, just maybe some Botox to stave off the eventual facelift, and then later a full head transplant.

Online I've already discussed my strong desire to become a MILF, and then later in life a GILF. It's a shallow goal, and I'm OK with that. I don't believe looks are everything, but perhaps I'm extra sensitive when it comes to my face. It's not that surprising, seeing as I film, edit, upload and watch myself regularly. Also, I'm still scarred from the disaster that was my eyebrows circa 2011–2015. I don't like to talk about it.

But seriously, I've reached a point in my life when I keep getting older. When did this start happening? Not only is it happening, but it's happening FASTER. I guess I just thought that it would never happen to me.

I'm fairly certain that the next step that comes with the ageing process is meant to be self-acceptance. But how can you accept something you are fundamentally against?! The weekend being extended by an extra day, now THAT'S something I could accept.

ROSE

Ageing is something we all embrace differently. Some of us fear it and some of us refuse point-blank to accept it. Perhaps I'll let myself go, shielded by the smokescreen of political standing, adamant that I don't feel obligated to look a certain way to remain attractive. I shall happily embrace my Edinburgh Woollen Mill collection, and will smell as interesting as beige looks, all in protest against society's perception of beauty. My breath won't necessarily suggest beauty comes from within, but that won't weaken my resolve (it might weaken other people's). Still, I'll wear my reversible fleece with pride paired with an ill-matching tunic, while storing the rest of my argument in the jowl pouches I choose not to surgically correct. Surely I'll be happy, knowing I never felt forced into filling my face with lies by creating cheeks where cheeks never were.

Or perhaps not.

Ageing doesn't bother me so much when I think about Rosie getting old and gross with me. I know exactly the kind of woman she wants to be. Oversized faux-fur coat, Hunter wellingtons, cashmere scarf, take-no-shit attitude, in a car playing hits from the nineties and parked on double yellow lines.

I always imagined I'd end up growing old in my art studio, with hair that resembled a small creature's habitat and oil paint still wet on my trousers. I'd be concentrating on my landscapes and have only one ear, because copying the greats is the ultimate form of flattery, and I imagine that Rosie's volume is only going to get louder. So reducing my hearing by 50 per cent should balance the scale. I'll want to pretend like I give a shit about potted plants, and will even grow my own vegetables, to cover in varnish and stick to thin air for my contemporary, conceptual period. I can't wait to journal my later years to pass on to my estranged children or a carer. I imagine it'll read something like this . . .

15 June 2058

I think Julio is after my fortune. I suspect he thinks that if he prunes the hawthorn he's entitled to a bonus, but I specifically told him to water the begonias and leave the hedges as they were, perfectly parallel.

Well, I woke up again today, which was a surprise. I'm almost certain it's my seventieth birthday. I lost track after my thirtieth, the last forty years have been somewhat of a blur. That could be my tequila breakfasts or the macular degeneration I inherited from my grandfather. Either way, times have certainly changed. Since the war of 2020, when the uprising of Kardashia left men politically powerless, the all-female administration split the men into twelve districts, from which a select few must fight to the death in a battle for equal pay and zero harassment. It's all live-streamed of course, for the entertainment of the Capitol, and is interactive to those with a subscription. It's on this afternoon in fact, so I look forward to a little birthday bloodshed with a sherry.

We haven't heard from Arabella since she told us she'd fallen in love with a man. Disappointing, but as a mother you have to think of their happiness first. I suspect she's living it up somewhere in Marbella in one of those straight-friendly bars they seem to congregate in. She tells me it's not a choice and that she was born that way, but she's young and impressionable and certainly not to be taken seriously. We had a disagreement and off she fled after an over-dramatic exchange of words, which caused tension between Rosie and me. I, of course, seem to be the bad cop, because I'm at the age when I do Sudoku and speak my mind. I was hoping to receive a card this morning, but Herbert hasn't brought me my mail so he's fired.

It's been a beautifully hot summer. All the polar icecaps have now melted and the rise in sea levels has destroyed problematic countries like Switzerland. Rosie and I have reserved our spot on Cloud 9 with TravelAfterlife, and I hear my mother's already reserved a sun *lounger up there, 'before the Germans could put their towels on them'. Everything is pretty idyllic: the sun is shining, the YouTube algorithm is faultless, and I think I can smell Rosie preparing expunged avocado on toast. I'd settle for smashed, but it is my birthday after all. Days like these make me miss bacon, but once veganism became religious doctrine it was harder to argue with.*

Rosie's aged badly. I haven't said anything because it's not constructive and would probably upset her. We hit thirty-five and she just gave up. Not through choice; her seventh father left and it was all downhill from there. Fortunately we found out he'd been selected for battle from District 10 and he didn't make it, which gave her closure.

We're still going strong. Our upload schedule isn't what it once was, but we're still making videos for the nine who watch. Technology certainly has developed since the days of Snapchat – President Blue Ivy Carter shushed that right up! When Branson was forced to sign his empire over to Kate Winslet, I think we were all sceptical about high-speed Virgin cruises of the North Atlantic, but the infrastructure had changed since 1912. It turned out to be exactly the break Rosie and I needed to reconnect. Not to each other, but to the internet. That summer our BT router was playing up, and all the male technicians were on strike demanding a close in the gender pay gap. The administration 'took care of them', of course, but it was tremendously inconvenient.

If there's anything I've learned in life, it's that the future is unpredictable. Look at Herbert. He had a job this morning and now he doesn't. If there's one thing I'll pass on to my alienated daughter, it's to appreciate every moment. Tomorrow you might wake up dead, or in her case heterosexual. So savour the good times.

ROSIE

Motherhood. It's something I simultaneously crave and am repulsed by. I come from a big family and the idea of an empty house terrifies me. Ditto the idea of spending every waking hour worrying about a miniature person. Rose and I do both see ourselves with children in the future, but, naturally, we have doubts, worries and questions. Questions like 'Does it go back to normal after the birth?' And 'Will my sex life be unaffected after pushing a human child out of my most precious area?' I'm not going to lie, the actual birth part is a huge fear factor in the whole process. Rose has a tilted pelvis and I have a squeamish nature and an overactive imagination. I've heard horror stories. I'd rather not be part of one.

We're not against the idea of adopting in the slightest. The concept of gaining a child pain-free *and* possibly helping to change someone's life for the better more than excites me. But having a child naturally would mean I had a tiny me to live vicariously through when I'm older, and a hasbian. The Spaughton genes are strong, and having a baby that would potentially look and act like me is a self-indulgent scenario I would like very much.

The problem with being in a same-sex relationship and wanting to have a child is that we can't just have a 'happy accident'. So Rose and I do feel the pressure to make sure everything is 'perfect' before we start the baby-making process. We set ourselves a rule that we would own a house before we started on whatever method we chose to have a baby. Well, we've bought the house; now I wish we could buy more time!

ROSE

I have so many questions about the future and the person I'm going to turn out to be. Should I have children for selfish reasons, because I'm worried I'll have no one to look after me when I'm old? Yes, though the truth is that doesn't really matter. There's no guarantee your children will like you enough to stick around, and chances are, you'll end up being looked after by one of the many Reese Witherspoons anyway, so why worry?

It's a question that often preys on my mind. Not Reese's entrepreneurial defiance of mortality, but the decision to have children.

There are so many benefits to having a baby. YouTube views, brand deals, self-importance, a Range Rover, exaggerated exasperation and opportunistic baby entitlement. But those aren't all the blessings children bring. You have the power to name another human being something entirely ostentatious, like Arrow or Flundermena, and egotistical baby privilege gives you a free pass to forget your manners. But until I become a yummy mummy, with all the credentials that qualify me for the status, I'll openly say that I hate them.

My experience of Hertfordshire mummies has been both inspiring and offensive. Inspiring in the sense that they've inspired me to believe their time is more precious than mine, and offensive in the sense that that offends me. In some respects I admire their matriarchal ubiquity. Their omnipresence and their ability to juggle their lives by executing the school run with military precision is impressive. But don't expect me to step aside to make room for your pram like it's your right. It's the life you chose. Yes, my dog ferociously barks at children; is that reason to assume she's dangerous? Probably, but what's more dangerous than an obnoxious child (with the small exception of natural disasters and a virus pandemic)? Their entitlement is beyond anything else I've experienced, and yummies are seemingly unavoidable. Whether they're stay-at-home yummies, work-from-home yummies or full-time-employment yummies, I'm done with the lot of them – until I unashamedly become one.

I recall a time I was waiting in line at the post office. I approached the window and asked which postal class would guarantee my item to arrive on time. A simple question with a straightforward answer. As the staff member explained what I needed, a yummy mummy who I could hear breathing directly behind me interrupted my conversation with 'Yeah, can I post my item while you're busy making all these decisions?'

I was triggered. Where did she get off thinking her time was the most valuable item in the post office? I turned around, shocked that anyone had such little patience, and angered by her rudeness. 'Decisions? I'm being served. It looks like you'll have to wait your turn.' She spat, hissed and grabbed her daughter's arm and dragged her out of the shop, mumbling something I couldn't quite hear as she left. But I made sure she heard me as I announced loudly how rude she was, appearing unbothered by her frustration and far less emotional than she was. A delicious serpent strike, if I do say so myself. What I wanted to ask her, had I more time, was why the big rush? Had she not time-managed efficiently? Was her husband not supportive enough, or was it all just getting a bit too much for her? Unforgivably sexist, but I know it would have angered the beast!

ROSIE

I've heard parents get extremely irritated when people compare having pets to having children. Why? If anything, children are ten times easier. You don't typically have to worry about them biting people, and you can drop them off at school, and leave them there. When we first got Wilma, our spoiled West Highland Terrier with attitude problems, she used to wake up in the night every two hours. We would get up and comfort her, feed her and clean up her mess. I don't see how that is in any way different to having a child. And children won't chew through your internet cables or the stems of your brand-new high heels.

Because we typically work from home, we figured we would be the best pet owners, because we wouldn't be leaving Wilma alone and unstimulated for hours every day. What it actually meant was that every time she barked, we were there to give her exactly what she wanted, and so she developed into the most demanding, manipulative dog you've ever met. My nightmare is raising a child I don't like. Nobody talks about stuff like that – why not?

But I do dream of Christmas with children, and watching them experience joy. Taking them to Disneyland, choosing their cute baby outfits to match my adult ensemble. Brushing their hair before school, reading them books, cuddling them, telling them how much I love them. I do think I have a huge maternal instinct just waiting inside of me.

I don't know any lesbian parents, probably because they all live in Brighton, but Rose and I have spoken to a few. One of our fears was that if we had children, they would be considered 'different' due to them having two mummies. But one lesbian mum assured me that it had actually given her children street cred. It made them 'cool' to come from a modern family. And if there's one thing any mother wishes for her child, it's that they're cool. That'll take them way further than initiative, creativity, passion or academic prowess.

ROSE

I don't know what kind of mother I'll be. Half of me wants to believe I'll be laid-back and liberal, but deep down I know I'm going to force upon them whatever I think is best – like higher education and sun cream. And they've met their match if they think I'll respond emotionally to any teenage backchat. I'll be unbeatable. They'll hate me for it at first, but I'll soon become their inspiration.

I can't imagine there would be much I wasn't prepared for. I don't mean in terms of sleepless nights and nappy changing – I'm absolutely not prepared for that. I mean in terms of emotional distress. 'Mum, I think I'm gay.' Yep, probably, you were raised by two women. 'Mum, I don't feel comfortable in this body.' Likely. Studies prove a balanced child needs to be raised by both a mother and a father. 'Mum, I'm being bullied.' Have you tried being something other than yourself? 'Mum, Timothy Dalton was the best Bond.' Get the fuck out.

See? Totally prepared.

However, that does raise the issue of hurting when your children are hurt. When my dog has an ear infection, I cry and bargain with the powers that be to remove the suffering in exchange for my own. If my child was getting picked on I'd be fully prepared to lose every inch of restraint and embrace the opportunity to defend them by systematically crushing the offenders, bypassing other parents and teachers with my own brand of anti-bullying vigilantism. I have a zero-tolerance policy when it comes to someone harming the people I love. It's my way or the highway. And by 'highway', I mean the lawful, less effective route.

ROSIE

Here's another fear: what if they like one mummy more than the other? Luckily, I have an advantage here. I'm not as crazy as Rose is about doing the washing-up or the hoovering, I am 100 per cent up for making a mess, and I love food that tastes good but is bad for you. Add to that my passion for children's films and I think I'm on to a winner, at least in the early stages of a kid's life. I will be totally unhelpful when it comes to maths homework, but hopefully I can get them into some good music.

Despite not yet being a parent myself, I still love to criticise others' parenting skills. And before you get mad, don't worry, I may dish it out but I can take it too. I'm eagerly anticipating the school-gate drama. I have some superficial aims: to be a hot mum is one of them. I imagine turning up early, outfit on fleek, home-made cake for the school bake sale, matching my outfit to my daughter's (whose name is Paris). The reality is that sometimes on a day off I don't even bother to wash. I have gone days in a row without brushing my hair, mostly when all I'm doing is sitting and editing, interrupted only by a few dog walks and dinner. No, I don't do my hair for the dog walk, OR for dinner. So my glam-orous motherhood dreams are just that: dreams.

I've been told that no amount of research and anticipation can prepare you for the actual reality that is motherhood. But I like to think I've watched enough 'Mummy Day in the Life' YouTube videos to know better. One exceptional advantage is that Rose and I are at home most days, whereas for most couples, one parent is alone while the other goes out to work. We're very, very lucky that there would be two of us on hand, or at least one of us while the other makes the coffee.

But do we actually want children right now? There was a time when I felt seriously broody, so broody that Rose was genuinely terrified. We'd always said that we wanted children in our future, and we decided that when we'd bought a house we would start exploring our options. Now that our house purchase has gone through, we aren't so sure. The deadline keeps getting pushed back. We've started thinking that we should enjoy our new house for a bit before we bring anyone else into it.

ROSE

The pressure to have children is unreal. Pressure from every angle. Motherhood doesn't come naturally to some, and as difficult as it might be to believe, it's not every woman's desire to become a parent. I already resent the idea of carrying something around for nine months when I've been carrying my emotional baggage around for twenty-nine years. I've eaten for two throughout my twenties, and the thought of total responsibility for another life alarms me like Pierce Brosnan alarmed the nation with his under-whelming singing ability. No one ever seems to talk about the possibility that you won't like your child. Don't get me wrong, I believe in the ability to love unconditionally, but on several condi-tions. One, don't take me for granted; and two, don't assume I'll carry you financially just because I carried you physically. Perhaps you've picked up on my negative tone towards parenthood, but maybe that's just because I've suddenly felt the pressure to make a decision.

I was never one to play with dolls. I had Puppy in my Pocket, Scalextric, the complete Playmobil zoo set, and the Playmobil ambulance in case there was an incident in the tiger enclosure. Whenever I played by myself I was never a mother. I was a father, a lion, or the president from *Independence Day*. I never aspired to have children; having a family was never something I gave much thought to. I'm wondering whether my maternal instinct will naturally kick in as I get older, but society seems to be trying to kick it in for me. So it's not so much a natural instinct as it is an expected one. And it doesn't just happen to me, it happens to a lot of women, especially in the workplace. The amount of times I've heard tales of men asking women when they plan on having a child, assuming firstly that they are able to have one, and secondly, that it's something that they want and should prioritise because 'time is running out'. Rude. Presumptuous and rude. There seems to be disapproval and bemusement directed at women who choose to focus on their careers rather than their families. It puzzles people. And as much as I wish I could deflect the pressure of these assumptions, instead I soak it up and spiral into a frenzy of thinking maybe I want to put myself first for now and freeze my eggs for later. If the worst comes to the worst, I'll place a bid on one of the Jolie-Pitts, but until that's been legalised I'm forced to make a decision on the right side of the law.

ROSIE

Despite how forward-thinking our society is becoming, I do still feel that there is an unspoken pressure to have children by a certain time. And I don't want to have a baby for the wrong reasons. Rose and I have surprised ourselves by deciding that there is a possibility that we will become mothers much later in our lives. Now, I've learned that life has a way of surprising you. I didn't plan a future with a wife and a shared business, it just happened that way and I'm more than pleasantly surprised. I didn't picture being an 'old' parent but that might happen too.

Rose and I have discussed putting off the family expansion process for a while, and there are many good reasons to do so.

Being frank, I'm currently in therapy and it would probably be a good idea not to need therapy just before putting my body through a huge hormonal change followed by a total life shift that involves an all-consuming job of protecting and caring for a life that's not my own. Also, I don't know if we're ready just yet. Add to that that our career is doing well and that there are still things I haven't done that I would like to do before settling down to have children. But you never know what will happen. Rose and I do want children. And I am feeling a little broody writing this.

ROSE

While visiting an animal sanctuary in Costa Rica, I learned about a particular breed of butterfly that lives for just three weeks before it dies. In that time their sole purpose is to reproduce and continue the cycle of creating life quickly followed by death. It really made me think. None of those butterflies had computer skills. None had explored their creative potential. None had a business model. I'm not saying they'd be able to get a business off the ground in three weeks, but it made me think, *What's the point?* Surely there's more to life than creating life? But maybe I'm approaching this wrong. Some say that you live your second life through your children. I have to admit, the idea of making Christmas magical for my babies in a world that can often seem dark brings me so much joy. And for me it doesn't matter whether or not I decide to have one naturally or whether we adopt. I believe that my children will always be my children, no matter how they're brought to me. Children are a gift. Unfortunately they don't come with a gift receipt for those just-in-case moments, but we can look beyond that and see them as miracles.

That's really all I have to say about the prospect of motherhood. I look forward to doing everything wrong.

How Would We Have Children?

ROSIE

So, how would we actually have children? We've narrowed down some of our options:

SAME SPERM, TWO PREGNANCIES

This was originally our first choice. This way we would each get to be a biological parent and by using the same sperm our children would be half-siblings. But there are issues with this method. What if one of us can't get pregnant, resulting in only one of us becoming a biological mother? What if one of us has twins and we don't want any more children? What if we freak out when we find out where babies come from?

EGG SWAP

I'm going to be honest, I'm not keen on this idea, even though I've seen couples do it successfully. This is when, for example, Rose would give me her fertilised egg and I would carry and birth the baby. It means that, on a technical level, we are both the child's biological mother. But things can go wrong. What if my body rejects Rose's egg? It's also extremely expensive. I understand why people do it, I'm just not sure it's for me.

FREEZING OUR EGGS

I feel so sci-fi when I consider this option. I love the idea: freezing them now so I still have the option to conceive a lot later in life. But it's expensive, and it doesn't guarantee anything, as the eggs have to survive the freezing process. Fertility on ice? Now there's a cocktail that's *not* virgin.

ADOPTION

Adoption is looking to be the likeliest of all the options, but I also know that I'm a Gemini with a decision-making problem. The problem is I can never decide. There are so many pros and cons to this route, but it's definitely something Rose and I would like to investigate further.

USING A SURROGATE

You know what they say, why do something yourself when you can pay someone else to do it for you? I'm just kidding. Look, I totally get why a surrogate is necessary in certain situations. But as far as we're aware, we're both capable of conceiving and birthing a child, so why would I make someone else do it if I'm not even sure if I want to? Saying that, Kim Kardashian has made it totally trendy now, so why not?

Parenting Troubleshooting by Rose & Rosie

All your parenting fears and concerns answered.

How do you know when it's hungry?
Duh, just ask it.

How should you react if your child tells you they hate you?
Take away their bed and give them a real reason to hate you.

What do you suggest if one child starts picking on the other?
Place a bet.

What if you like one child more than the other?

Having more than one child is a fantastic way to spend extra time relaxing. Send your least favourite to do your daily tasks for you and maximise your binge-watching.

What should you do if you drop your child?

What Britney did. Nothing. Instead, focus your attention on your comeback album. Millions of dollars tend to soften the blows that any lack of love or care during infancy might have inflicted. Money will fix everything, including superficial wounds, if applied correctly.

What should you do if you suspect your child of bullying other children at school?

Tell them they inherited their aggression from their father.

Do I need to sterilise bottles and pacifiers after every single use?

No. Forget what those overly cautious nurses said at antenatal class. I've let my dog chew on a pacifier plenty of times before giving it back to the child who dropped it, and it's never been a problem. Your child will be fine – if anything, dirt will boost their immune system.

I can't get my child to latch on when breastfeeding and I'm close to giving up. Does this make me a bad parent?

Yes. Tell me, did you plan on raising a quitter?

What constitutes 'sleeping through the night', and will it ever happen?
Listen, if you can't recognise when your own baby is sleeping through the night you were never cut out to be a parent. Please send it back immediately.

Is green poop normal?
Not if it's yours. Back away from the juicer.

My toddler throws tantrums in public . . .
Here's the thing, children learn by watching. So who's really to blame?

30 things to do before you're 30 – by Rosie Spaughton

From a twenty-something who already knows everything.

1. Go on a Britney Spears-esque road trip across America with your girlfriends, *Crossroads* style. Figure out if you are in fact still a girl, or simply not yet a woman. Find yourself, and along the way, find the perfect trilby to complement all your other perfect features. Cheat on Justin Timberlake. Think about having children later on and then dropping them.

2. Take a risk. This could be something as simple as marrying Kevin Federline, or as deep as pitching a TV series set in a dystopian yet historic Western future with robotic hookers and a self-playing piano. Maybe create yet another TV streaming service, despite the serious competition.

3. Get a tattoo. Why not? Why merely admire the art in various galleries when you could permanently attach it to your own skin and get bored of it quicker? The possibilities are endless.

4. Bungee jump. Why sit at home and wait for death when you could get out there and carpe diem yourself!

5. Start a collection. I'm already way ahead of the game, I've been collecting various-sized hearts and bogies since the late nineties. Sometimes Rose collects her toenails in a little pile on her bedside table. It's extremely well organised.

6. Eat really expensive food, because I'm told rich people's stuff is better. Why burn your money when you could eat it? Count calories rather than pounds. Wait a second . . .

7. Go and watch some kind of sport live, even if you aren't interested, just so you can take a selfie and make a splash online, in a desperate bid to appear cool and retain your cultural relevance.

8. Pee in all twenty-two of the world's oceans. The world is your massive, gross-tasting oyster.

9. Learn a new language, OR, in my case, make up your own to prevent people from reading your diary. Then, forget how to read it and spend the rest of your days trying to interpret your chicken scrawl entry about that murder mystery party, so you can *finally* have closure that it wasn't you.

10. Invest all your savings into stocks that will *never* plummet, like lip-filler buoyancy aids, the latest mode of time travel or the male contraceptive pill.

11. Similar to number 10, and also to number 2, take a risk and invest your life savings into a start-up business with your best friend. NOTHING could go wrong.

12. Sleep with your straight best friend, regardless of your own sexuality. The awkwardness will either bring you closer or will cull a dead-end friendship. Win win!

13. Make mistakes that subsequently become regrets. This will help you later in life if you feel like becoming a scarred superhero with a back story, or even a misunderstood and relatable villain that just went too far down the wrong path. This will also help with: wearing a leather jacket, brooding, drinking at a bar alone, drinking whisky neat without wincing, sitting in the dark, staying awake at night, closing yourself off from any form of relationship and distancing yourself from others.

14. Waste your spare time coming up with perfect retorts to all the friends you argued with circa 2005 onwards. Or even better, during your school years. This will help your life pass by quicker without your having to be productive or achieving anything apart from bitterness and resentment! Ladies, those grudges won't hold themselves!

15. Become a Hollywood icon, but peak too soon. That

way you can spend the rest of your life drinking and retelling the same stories from forty years ago on one of your endless stints on reality television. Overcome your addiction and write your fourth memoir. Marry Geri Halliwell.

16. Test your limits and personal boundaries and do something that scares you. This could push your fear into a fully fledged phobia, leading you to seek therapy. Have an affair with your hot older therapist who just so happens to be questioning her sexuality. Discover that she's been breaking the codes of conduct by stalking her patients and cut off the relationship. Realise that the one time you tested your fear two years ago has now come full circle and that you are stronger because of it. Create a TV series about your ex-therapist's life that later gets cancelled. Realise you are completely healed.

17. Improve your wine knowledge so you can become a wine cunt.

18. Get to know your family history so you can discover the shocking secret that the first dad who left was actually not your real dad at all, but in an unexpected twist of events and due to sheer mathematical chance, you uncover that your biological father was in fact the seventh father to leave. Fascinating.

19. Find your true purpose. Is it acting? Yoga? Adopting rescue dogs or working for charities abroad? Fuck your true purpose and marry a prince.

20. Become the inventor of something iconic. For example, after my career on YouTube ends I plan to become a full-time 'back-seat driver', something me and my friend just started up. It's when people hire you to correct them when they are driving just fine. Requirements are weak eyesight and a dogmatic attitude.

21. Make discoveries, about yourself and the rest of the world. For example, discover a new continent.

22. If you can't already, learn to speak Spanish. It's estimated that more than 470 million people speak Spanish as a native language. But if you want something even MORE useful, learn how to speak a much less common language, like Njerep, which is spoken exclusively by four people in Nigeria. This will give you the ability to always say exactly what's on your mind with the minimum chance of offending anyone. Get a friend to learn it with you, so you can bitch about the rest of the world freely.

23. Take a spontaneous trip alone to find yourself. Go to the airport with nothing but your passport and get the next flight to anywhere. Forget clothes, you can buy them at your destination, even though you won't be prepared by having the correct currency or a suitcase to put them in. I promise this will be the least stressful trip you'll ever make. Attempt to document your journey, despite not having a camera. Don't tell anyone where you are or what you're doing. But most of all, have fun!

24. Move to a new city. Change your name. Become someone else. Realise you've become your mother.

25. Go to Las Vegas and learn how to gamble. What better way to spend your money than on a game of chance? Lose money but gain an addiction to gambling.

Gamble with your future. Congratulate yourself: you are now officially a risk-taker.

26. Go skinny dipping! What's more freeing than nudity in public places? One time I was sunbathing topless and noticed an old man I didn't know standing very near to me, watching. New experiences are fun!

27. Show the world your creativity. Release an album or write a book. It must be easy or else the YouTubers wouldn't be doing it!

28. Go on a silent retreat. Have conversations, meet new people.

29. Meet your idol. Find a way. Laws are there to be broken.

30. And finally, fail spectacularly at something, mope around for a bit, and then try again and again until you hit success, all while listening to the same backing track. This provides the *perfect* cinematic montage of your character development, if ever you became famous and need to make a blockbuster hit about your life.

ROSE

My ambitions for the future often change. Not that I'm flighty with fleeting goals, but with each day I seem to re-evaluate what's important to me. Perhaps that's just what happens as you grow: the things that used to feel important shift and seem less significant. When I was younger I couldn't wait to be older – all the independence that would come with adulthood, the opportunity to become someone, the cars and the women that would inevitably accompany a quarter-life or midlife crisis, it all seemed so hopeful. Now, my ideal future is one when I can spend as much time with my family as possible. I really love my mum and dad, and the thought of losing them frightens me more than anything. More than clowns, more than the outcome of running with scissors, more than a Stephanie Meyer cameo. It genuinely keeps me awake at night, and a small part of me even believes there's something I can do to stop it from happening. Which would be ridiculous if I weren't such a talented problem solver with access to higher beings.

Losing my parents will be an event in my life that I'll never feel ready for, yet I constantly try to accept. Unlike my younger self, now, when I think about my goals for the future, I think about the quality of my relationships. I want to know everything there is to know about my parents, so that I can achieve a true sense of closeness before they ascend to the afterlife and argue about the draught Mum can feel on her cloud. I want to live my life knowing I've spent my time on things that are truly important. I think it's stupid to say that money can't buy you happiness – it absolutely can. You can find happiness simply by having financial stability. However, for me it's time that I value the most. Time, and relationships.

I hate to sound pessimistic, and it's only because I'm constantly on high alert, but when I look to the future I worry about losing the people in my life. So one of my goals is to have no regrets and to make time for the people I love. I don't want to live a life wishing I'd done something differently after it was too late. When you strip life down, it's the people you share it with that bring the most happiness. And as cheesy as it sounds, being happy is often goal enough and is not always achievable depending on your circumstances. Ten years ago my biggest goal for the future was to stay alive. Now my biggest goal is to make the most of the time I have with the people who have loved and supported me through my darkest times.

I'm also trying to do one good deed a day. I want to leave a positive mark on the world, not necessarily because I care for other people, but because it makes me feel great about myself. No, in all seriousness, what are we other than our actions? Although I will say that it's difficult to find a good deed that is entirely selfless. Even the prospect of feeling good about yourself directly benefits you! But surely if two people are benefiting that's even better than one? My good deeds range from not booby-trapping the fridge so things fall on Rosie when she opens it to offering my seat to a serpent on the Tube. That one was particularly hard to swallow. We both beelined for the one empty seat available, and girlfriend was NOT going to back down. When we both reached that holy grail of peak travel time, she looked at the seat, then back at me with a face that screamed, *Feigned moral conundrum! Whatever shall we do!* I knew she had no intention of letting me have it, so to avoid tension, I kindly offered it to her. Before I could finish my sentence she'd already sat down, barely giving a word of thanks. I added that to my daily list of good deeds, but it was soon negated when I stole her purse.

I think it's a great way to live your life. Not crime, but trying to make decisions that benefit others. I'm a strong believer in the butterfly effect, and if I can positively influence the events of someone's day, I'm going to take that opportunity, then let it develop into a moral superiority complex that makes me conceited and unlikeable.

When you're young time passes by so slowly and suddenly you've reached fourteen and have to start picking your GCSEs, then your A levels, then your degree subject if you choose to carry on studying. You have to choose the course of your life fairly early on, and you're advised to be realistic in the ambitions you have and the choices you make. Having a dream or an ambition is often mocked or seen as unrealistic, and some of us are so embarrassed to talk about our aspirations that we end up too afraid to pursue them. But life moves fast even when it feels like it's taking for ever. One thing I see in my future is that I'll continue to have highly ambitious targets. I want to win an Oscar, I want to initiate an artistic move-ment, I want the Nobel Peace Prize, I want a talk show, a Netflix series, a porcupine defence mechanism – the list is endless. I want to see everything and go everywhere and I believe I can do it all. I've done so much I never thought I was capable of, so I'll continue to push myself in the years to come and follow the fear.

Positive Manifestation and Shaping Our Future

ROSIE

Positive manifestation. Something I've talked about extensively with my therapist. I believed in it, then I gave up on it, and then I believed in it again.

Being an extremely spiritual person, I really believe that the power of our thoughts can affect the world around us. And as a renowned professor of theoretical thinking, I'm also interested in the facts and evidence behind it. Is it real? Can thinking good thoughts attract good things to you? And if so, what does it then mean if you are having a bad day? Will a bad mood attract bad luck? Does it mean it's actually my fault that my dad left when I was three? Had I been in a perma-nent bad mood for three years, and was it that negativity that caused him to run away and find a new family? And if so, does it mean that his new family are more positive-thinking than I am, and that's the reason he's stuck around?! I'm spiralling.

But writing these thoughts down as they come into my head only serves to demonstrate how many questions the concept of positive manifestation raises.

On the off chance that you are reading this book and are not a millennial (or perhaps you're just out of touch), positive manifestation is the notion that when you think positive thoughts, you attract positive situations into your life. And vice versa: if you think negative thoughts, you encourage negative situations.

When I first found out about this, being the impressionable and eager person I am, I was excited to try it out, and, like most people naturally would, I tried to think positively about winning the lottery. I had a few family members who could have really done with the money at the time, and also, who wouldn't want to buy themselves their own yacht and name it *Princess Beyacht*?

I thought long and hard about winning the lottery, imagining what I'd spend the money on and how happy my family would be when they were finally freed from their financial burdens. And then, on an extremely good day, when the sun was shining and Rose and I were taking a break from a weekend Netflix binge with a dog walk, I got an email. I had won the lottery!

The email said:

Dear Rosie,
We have some news about your ticket from the draw
on Saturday 23rd September 2017. Please sign into
your account as soon as you can for more information.
Congratulations, and thank you for playing.

I had won! Sure, I had only won £25.00, but I'd still won. I'd never won before. Positive manifestation worked and this was all the proof I needed to believe in it!

I got sucked into watching YouTube videos about the subject for further tips and advice. People said, 'You must be specific and write down clear goals.' I realised that I had manifested winning the lottery, but I had never said how much I wanted to win. It was all making more and more sense to me.

But then things started to get difficult. I started to panic if I ever had a negative thought. I'd think, *Oh my God, stop thinking about that right now or more bad things will happen. Oh my God, I'm thinking about not thinking about it which means I'm still really thinking about it!* If something negative came up, I didn't want to address it, I just wanted to keep being positive. But sometimes things happen in life that you can't just breeze past with a smile, like when my second dad left. And people have worse things happen to them, like illness, or death, or homelessness. Can this really be why all the good and bad things happen in the world? Because of our thoughts? The whole thing was driving me crazy. If I spoke badly about someone, would it come back to bite me three times as bad? Did it make me a bad person if I had a nasty thought? I started to police my own thoughts, heavily berating or judging myself if every single thing I said or did wasn't perfectly well intended.

This is where my hot therapist comes in again. She told me there's no such thing as luck or magical thinking. 'How do *you* know?' I pouted. She might be hot but does that mean she has all the answers? Yeah, probably, but I still had to question her. She told me about studies that had been done about positive manifestation, luck, and good things happening to people. They found that the people who had good things in their life or who regularly won things tended to try more, and the more often you try at something, the more likely you are to win, or to succeed. Even if you fail and try again, you probably learned some tricks from the first time around and so will have an even better chance.

She also explained that superstitions come from common sense. For example, if you walk under a ladder and someone is standing on the ladder working, there's a greater chance that something will fall on you, like a pot of paint or the weight of a human being. Nothing to do with luck.

Although I still questioned her logic, it did make sense to me. But I realised something. Even if there was no such thing as 'magical thinking' (making something happen with the power of your thoughts), positive manifestation *had* been magical for me. By being positive, I hadn't let things bother me as much. I had felt confident that every problem had a solution. I'd felt calmer, believing that everything would work out for the best. I saw the good in everything.

What I now realised was that the power of our thoughts *can* positively shape our future. But it's not our future we are changing, it's our way of looking at it. I'm not saying you have to feel happy all the time – in fact I learned quite the opposite. Your thoughts are just that – thoughts – and it's OK to feel sad or to feel negative emotions. Nothing will happen as a result. But with a positive outlook, maybe you can make something incredible materialise.

What I'm learning is that life goes by in a flash – and Rose and I are so lucky to have it all on camera. Recently, a viewer wanted me to react to an old video, in which we'd answered the question 'Where do you think you'll be in five years' time?' Well, I had predicted that Rose and I would get married, and sure enough, five years have passed and we've been married for three of them. This got me thinking: where do I predict I'll be five years from now?

If my mathematics is correct, five years' time brings us to the year 2023 (or later, depending on when you are reading this book). Ideally, my roots won't need doing and there won't be visible plaque build-up on my gnashers. I'd love to think that I'll still have a lovely warm home to live in, a soft bed to sleep in, a wife and two fur babies to snuggle. Perhaps I will be pregnant? Actually, I think we may already have children by then. Or even better, they'll have invented zero-calorie ice cream and Rose will have finally said yes to the fluffy pink soft furnishings of my dreams!

ROSE

It's difficult to predict what the future will bring, but I imagine it'll go a little like this . . .

25 February 2023

I hate Rosie's fluffy pink soft furnishings. Five years have passed since we wrote that bestseller, and Rosie has spent all of the money we made on fluffy wallpaper with a leopard-print trim. She said it comple-mented her personality and moved with the wind. We're indoors. Her roots really need doing and there's a distinct build-up of plaque on her teeth. Our mattress is hard and our home is freezing. She's eaten so much full-fat ice cream lately that the wallpaper is starting to move with her lactose intolerance.

Despite all that, we're having a baby. We've both decided that Rosie will carry it. I'll birth it, but Rosie will carry it after it's born as I usually carry the car keys and most of the shopping. And what's life if not a balance? I was nervous at first at the prospect of naturally giving birth to a child – surely that's like forcing a lemon through a Slush Puppy straw? But it's not so much the physicality of it all that's troubling me. After a long, arduous discussion and a game of rock, paper, scissors, we've settled on a donor. We tried to find genes most like Rosie's father, to make sure he'll want no involvement or any legal rights to our child. I'm not really sure what happens next. The doctors say I'll need to be inseminated, so I imagine it'll be an oral procedure or a cream of some sort and then WHAM! Pregnant. Fingers crossed, anyway!

But what if it's twins? They run in my family. Some walk, but most of them want to get places faster than the other twin, especially if there's food around. I'm not sure we can handle two tiny infants. Rosie can't even catch a tennis ball when it's stationary. What if one of them eats the other one in a survival of the fittest? What if they can't tell the difference between their sibling and their own reflection so they bark at both? What if they inherit Rosie's IQ through their environmental upbringing?

Twins or no twins, we've thought of a few names. Rosie wants Paris for a boy or girl so I told her to fuck off. Not much goes with Dix, but I like Chase or Isaac for a boy – either will garner far less unwanted attention than a name inspired by location. You have to think about what school will be like for them, and no one likes a Paris. A Paris will cling on to hope when romantic feelings aren't returned, and they're always boasting about square footage. I don't even like Paris as a city, so I probably won't like it as my child.

We're decorating the nursery in gender-neutral colours so the internet thinks we care about that stuff. YouTube will contribute to our baby's college fund, so we have to make sure we're tapping the right demos. Views have been dropping off lately, probably because I've run out of bisexual jokes and Rosie's run out of stupid questions – something none of us foresaw. Now is the perfect time to start a family so we can introduce a new dynamic to our videos. I just hope I can afford help if I need it. How am I going to juggle a baby? I'll need a second and a third object, and juggling infants for views will surely be demonetised but it's content I'd certainly subscribe for. Perhaps someday I'll be rich enough to employ a gardener, but right now I need to prioritise childcare. I'd ask my mum but she's on a thirty-six-month cruise to Vietnam. I'd ask Laura but she'd probably micro-manage the baby and try to feed it a pie chart. I'd ask John but he's in prison for identity fraud. Sigh.

We'll be fine. I'm excited to hear what our baby's first word will be and whether it's pronounced correctly. I hope it loves me more. Surely if I breastfeed it'll see me as the fountain of life and Rosie as a stagnant dormant well? I worry they'll have a better relationship with each other than I do with either of them and that I'll be cast aside the way Flynn was when he became boring and invaluable to the channel. But these are probably unsubstantiated worries. For now I look forward to motherhood. You can't spell motherhood without 'hero' and that's exactly what I plan to be! Then again you can't spell it without 'doom' either, so maybe we're fucked.

Questions About the Future

If you could ask your seventy-year-old self one question, what would it be?

What's the difference between 'affect' and 'effect'?

If you could live anywhere, where would you live?

Miami, Seattle, New York, Costa Rica or, if I were to throw in a wild card, Carmarthen.

If you made a time capsule now what would you put in it?

My defensive sarcasm. I'll need that when I'm old and resentful of the youth.

What do you predict your post-retirement hobby will be?

Not dying, closely followed by competitive table tennis.

What advice would you give your elderly self, based on your experience of life so far?

Never forget that everyone else is wrong.

What do you predict your midlife crisis indulgent purchase will be?

A divorce settlement OR a start-up Italian restaurant chain catering to tough neighbourhoods, called Spaghetto.

Which family member do you plan on dropping?

Whoever sells their story first.

If you could create a new social platform, what would it be?

MooTube. YouTube for cows.

If you could implement one worldwide change, what would you do?

For straight girls to stop queer-baiting their gay friends and breaking their hearts.

Who do you think will die first out of you and Rosie?

Well, Rosie's blonde and bisexual so if life was a horror film, it would be her. She's also the type who'd run towards danger in a fit of Google Maps confusion. In the event that I go first, leaving her with another ten to fifteen years on her own, I expect she'll temporarily mourn then relocate to Aspen. She doesn't know where that is, but I know the intrigue will get the better of her because it sounds racy and suggestive and bisexuals love all that, don't they.

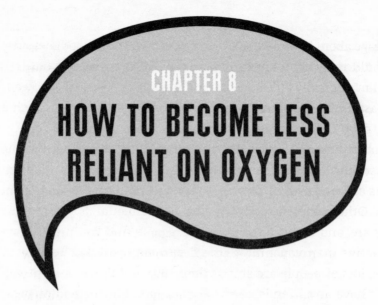

CHAPTER 8

HOW TO BECOME LESS RELIANT ON OXYGEN

'Until Ellen Page says it… it becomes so.'

ROSIE

OK, guys, we've reached the final chapter, so make yourself a cup of tea and grab some Doritos because it's about to get juicy. After a year of writing this book we've lost all our inhibitions and we're tired of beating about the bush. Not that I have one any more since laser hair removal, but regardless: it's time to overshare.

As an avid reader myself, I would suggest that a book's final chapter should be a culmination of everything you have previously learned throughout the book being put to excellent use in a climactic finale. But I'm afraid all we can offer you is a checklist and an experimental new sandwich filler. I kid! This chapter is going to be jam-packed with useful information!

(Sandwich idea: Super Noodles between bread, aka the 'Carb de la Carb'. You're welcome.)

As we usually round off our live tours and YouNow streams with our 'Advice of the Week', we decided we'd throw in some ad hoc suggestions that might help you on your way. And of course, it wouldn't be a Rosie Spaughton book if I didn't express my outrage about biphobia, so I've chucked that in for good measure! I would mention what Rose plans on covering in this chapter, but I'm not really talking to her at the moment because she keeps Instastorying me going to the toilet in hopes that she'll catch a plop drop. Content at its finest, but also grounds for divorce.

I'm just going to kick this chapter off with some comforting reassurance. No one remembers that stupid thing you said ten years ago, and even if they do, they aren't thinking about it right now. Other people usually aren't as judgemental as you assume they are, and I have a feeling other people find you much more attractive than you find yourself. No one really knows how to cook, lots of people are shit at their jobs and don't worry if you don't have any friends, everyone dies alone in the end anyway, and if you want to eat that thing, eat that thing. That is all.

ROSE

Wow. Rosie, you've really left me shaken with that profound summing up.

It's here. The chapter where everything comes together in a perfect epiphany. Where everything you've read leads you to a moment of realisation, of understanding. A moment when we finally become enlightened or conscious of something. But of what? Perhaps you've realised it's only possible to low-five a penguin, or maybe you're beginning to question whether cereal is just cold soup? Maybe it's even something a little more related to this book. After 80,000 words I'm sick of my own inner monologue. I'm even more sick of Rosie's, but those aren't the only things I've learned.

I've learned that you and I have commonalities that reach far beyond a similar sense of humour. I've only come to realise it now, but I've been writing this book with me in mind. I don't mean my royalty percentage, but my younger self. I've spoken about the trials and tribulations life's had to offer in hopes that my experiences could offer some kind of relief to anyone fighting similar demons.

The fact is we all have them. But remember who's in charge. You. Or your wife . . . it really depends who wears the trousers, and as we all know, in every lesbian relationship one of you is the man. But like bisexuals, demons can be tamed. You can be the puppeteer of your own imps, if given the right strings!

I plan to cover a lot in this concluding chapter. Some of it will be discussed sardonically for extra bants, but you'll know when I'm being serious. This journey has been therapeutic in the sense that I've been able to share my biggest secrets and discuss what I deem to be the most shameful parts of myself. But you know what they say, a problem shared is a problem halved – or magnified by a thousand if shared with my mother. I take that back. Mum, you did *not* overreact when I came in from school inexcusably drunk with unidentified excrement down my blazer. You reacted like any mother would. With care and slight force.

I've realised exactly what this chapter needs and what I'd want out of it if I were one of you guys. Nudes. Scrap that, the publisher will hate it. Or LOVE it, but I couldn't put 'author' in my Twitter bio in good conscience if this book didn't have some credibility. Not that people who decide to share nudes aren't credible . . . I sense thin ice. I'm moving on before someone's outraged. Here's a quick tip (and there are many more to follow): if you sense you've said something inadvertently offensive or ignorant, quickly preoccupy their minds with a riddle.

What goes up, but never comes down, is wet
when dry, has wings but cannot fly?

Now, there's no answer to this riddle (unless it's somehow Nicolas Cage), but your accuser now has a new problem to deal with. The outrage that you'd inspired has been replaced and temporarily forgotten. In this cooling-off period you can make sure you coun-teract your mistake with some distracting, charitable tweets, or, if needs be, a YouTube apology video beginning with a sigh and a title exculsive to lower-case lettering. Then announce that all the AdSense revenue from the video will be donated to a charity of the accuser's choice (but don't follow up with receipts – no one ever cares enough to follow up).

In the age of outrage culture, you can avoid being the subject of outrage by presenting a bigger outrage. I wouldn't suggest not being problematic in the first place, because that's nowhere near as interesting, is it? And no one's ever fallen from grace without hugely profiting from it, am I right?

I think this would be a good time to throw in some tips about how to make it as a YouTuber, but before we do, how is my sarcasm translating? Well? Can you imagine if people don't realise I'm trolling, and the Amazon reviews that could follow?

Overshare is a classic example of an uneducated influencer abusing their position and encouraging their audience to be problematic and combative. Dix's lack of writing experience is evident from start to finish and her wife should stick to gnawing on a crayon.

Rose is OK but I can't understand what the other one is saying. It's like white noise jumping from the page every time she writes anything. It sheds light on the failure of the education system.

Sick of YouTubers capitalising off this trendy 'self-love' era. If you need to earn that coin, go get a real job and stop exploiting people.

Talk about tapping that demo. Nicely done girls.

I bought this book for the cover. The inside is shit.

This formula of trumping an issue with a bigger issue is one my mum uses whenever I come to her with a problem. It's her method of ensuring my issues don't escalate.

'God, I haven't been sleeping well, Mum.' 'Well, I haven't slept in years!'

'I keep getting these niggling headaches . . .' 'Well, my migraines have been absolutely AWFUL recently.'

'I've been feeling a little stressed lately . . .' 'Yes, well, I'm having a breakdown.'

You see? My problem has already been reduced by hearing about my mum's bigger problem. It's a technique guaranteed to be successful. There's nothing more distracting than the idea of a larger calamity. I could barely remember my own troubles after hearing my mum's, which, as you can see, were much worse. So if you take anything from this book, remember: distraction is everything. Whether it's a riddle, a conundrum or a greater concern, throw it straight into the mix. If you insult someone, bring to light other social justice issues, though preferably someone's else's wrong-doings, to avoid negative attention.

If you bought this book in hopes that we'd offer some genuine creator advice, here it is. All of the tips below will help you grow your audience and keep you relevant. It's not as easy as it might look to create entertaining original content every week, so here are a few things that will boost your social-media profile across all platforms.

1.   Be problematic and then point the finger at someone else. As explained above, draw enough attention to yourself to be the topic of conversation, but if that attention becomes damaging, abort with a separate smear campaign. Don't worry if you start trending with the hashtag #yournameisoverparty. Use your business acumen to turn this situation into profit by creating a board game where the aim is to fight social-justice warriors (and vegans) to clear your name and rid the internet of outrage culture. It's likely to sell out, and when it does, become problematic all over again and enjoy the rollercoaster of online stardom.

2.   Stay in your room. Form friendships over social media and keep them there. Real-life friendships are time-consuming; and remember, never leave the house.

3.   Get involved in stan wars. Stan accounts can have big follow-ings. Be sure to align yourself with the biggest, no matter who they're supporting. Demi Lovato has one you're going to want in on. If ever there's an explosion of 'stantosterone', pour fuel on the fire and put yourself on the map. You'll be seen as a leader amongst many, a 'queen' for 'supporting another queen', but most importantly, the influx of followers will be worth the extra work.

4.   Google yourself. Stumble across chat forums and relish reading what everyone else is saying about your competitors. Anonymously contribute to the negativity, and then search for your own page. Allow yourself to fall to pieces for five minutes, pull yourself together and film a reaction video. Be sure to give websites like these exposure to encourage a gossip archive for future content.

5.   Tweet incessantly about how you're 'ridding yourself of toxic energy' and allowing 'positive vibes only'. You're sure to attract teenagers at the peak of their angst!

6.   Post revealing photographs 'by accident' and swiftly remove them. Nothing beats whetting the appetite with a premeditated appetiser! If you're going down the semi-nudity route, don't give away too much or you risk having nothing to rely on when you need it in the future. And everyone knows nudity is the best controversy! Especially if you're female and under scrutiny. Men, you'll be seen as studs. Women, you'll be seen as sluts. So get your-self a 'momager' and own that label.

7.   Pay the paparazzi to take flattering 'candid' shots to stay relevant. This is one of my favourites and is a surefire way to stay at the top of your game. It's worth the minor expense to be snapped around London as the wind delicately brushes that one strand of hair across your face, allowing the world to see that you 'just woke up like this'.

8. Moderately clickbait and work your way up. You can't jump in full throttle. You have to build trust before you can decide to abuse it.

9. Find a 'hook' to rely on. I'm gay so I'm untouchable. Any criticism I receive can be counterargued and rebuffed by my gaylord shield. Find whatever works for you, even if it's simply coming from Norwich. Use it, abuse it, don't lose it.

10. Mock yourself before others can. There are two benefits to this. Number one: self-deprecation is incredibly chic. Give off that sweet-but-shy vibe, because it resonates strongly with Generation Z. You'll do well on Tumblr with it, just don't forget to add #awkward because being awkward is this season's strongest trend. It's like the military-style jacket – it's timeless. Number two: by mocking yourself you take the power away from other people doing it to you, leaving them unable to repeat what you've already said, rendering their opinions useless and ineffective. Note that I've already written negative reviews of this book IN THIS BOOK. Do what I do when I expect criticism and take the piss out of how shit, sexist, offensive or unfunny your content is. Do it with a sprig of humour and irony and it totally prevents other people from being able to echo your words. No one can argue with irony: you've already made their point for them – ironically! You've beat them to the punch!

11. Spread false drama. If you're feeling desperate for new ideas, fabricate events and create false drama. Outrage spreads like wildfire and we care little for checking sources. If something has more than 10K retweets on Twitter it's automatically true. Whether you're tarnishing your own name for attention or dragging someone else, just make sure it's juicy. It doesn't even have to be believable. This is the age of consumption – we'll believe anything if it's a trending hashtag!

12. Get a puppy. Everyone knows this is the most desperate card to play, before having a baby. It provides you with content that's cute and unpredictable. This new addition also gives you a story arc. But make sure you 'adopt don't shop' or at least appear as though that's what you've done. Get a breed that can fit into bags and can be dressed up. Big dogs only do well on Instagram when it snows. They don't fit into frame when it comes to shooting videos, so take that into account.

13. Collaborate. Our channel is FULL of collaborations. When we spot someone on the rise, we'll capitalise off them by introducing ourselves to their audience. So take advantage of other people's hard work because it's the only way to grow on the platform. Support bigger YouTubers by kissing ass. They'll know you're doing it but they love it anyway, and you never know what doors it might open!

14. Do an ad for Audible or Best Fiends. Now you're officially a fully fledged YouTuber!

This journey has been a long one. Not just because we extended our first draft deadline, but because it's initiated personal growth. I can't remember the person I was twelve months ago when we started this process, but I'm loving the person I am now. Older, a little more weathered, chiselled from stress, but in an attractive, Hugh Jackman way. I've decided to ask Rosie a few questions about her own experience writing the book, not because I'm interested but because I've got to hit our word count somehow.

In Chapter 6 I notice you mentioned having a profound respect for the environment. How do you feel knowing you could have just published an e-book instead of a paper one?

Books can be recycled, Rose. Only you wouldn't know anything about that because a) you don't read and b) you don't recycle.

I don't read yet my vocabulary is as extensive as your history with men. Strange! So, during your frequent times of procrastination, what was your first port of call?

Checking my Sims were still planting watermelons to earn as much money as possible in order to build my dream pink Sims house. Playing *Fortnite* and bitching about you in my diary were also up there amongst my top priorities.

I'll be sure to give it a read. What do you think your father would say if he ever read this book?

He never read my texts, so I can only dream that my father would take enough interest in me to read my book.

Did you ever consider dedicating it to him for lols?

No, but I did consider dedicating it to my unborn child, Paris.

What one thing did you learn about yourself during this process?

That after spending many hours sitting looking down at my iPad I've begun to develop a turkey gobbler.

If there was one thing that you've mentioned in this book that you fear you might regret later, what would it be?
Hmmm. I'm not sure I've written anything I regret. Shall I write something regrettable now just for fun? Let's see . . . One time a boyfriend requested that I poop on his chest, and I tried my hardest but I just didn't need to go. Looking back, I'm astounded by my commitment and the amount of effort I went to for him.

I commend your decision to publish that. If you weren't already a fan of our YouTube channel, would you now be inclined to subscribe? Because I would.
Yes, and I would also hit that notification bell for good measure, just to make sure that all updates went into my sub box.

What's been your favourite chapter?
I like all the chapters but particularly I favour Chapter 5 and onwards, because that's when I started working in a separate room from you and it made the whole process ten times less annoying. In case you didn't quite catch that, I was insinuating that you were the problem.

Right. So which charity are you going to donate 100 per cent of the book's proceeds to?
The charity called my mortgage.

Have you intentionally thrown shade at any point in this book?
Yes, but I've written and edited so much now that I can't remember what I've kept in and what I've cut. But yes: I

hate people and I'm bitter, so I hope that comes across in my writing.

When the novelty wears off, will you use the book as a doorstop or as a coffee-table talking piece?
When the novelty wears off I will write another book. You can't spell 'novelty' without 'novel', Rose.

Will you send the book to YouTubers you never talk to in hopes that they'll promote it on their social media?
Yes, but purely to see if the people who I have promoted books for will return the favour by promoting mine. If they don't, there's going to be some serious WhatsApp group bitching going on. Plus I'll bitch about them in my next book, *Novelty*.

If you write a second book, will you reveal that you eat meat or do you think that's too controversial?
That's probably too controversial. I was going to wait until I became pregnant so I can blame my unethical and selfish meat consumption on my unborn child's needs.

Could this book ever be dramatised for television or does it not have enough substance?
It could, but one of us would be killed off.

Are you happy with the RRP price?
I can hand on heart say that I don't know what the RRP is! But I've spent a year of my life writing this so the RRP better be good. You can't spell RRP without R and R.

ROSE

OK, Rosie, now I'm ready to answer YOUR questions. Hit me with the good stuff and I'll be as honest as I can!

Did you actually write this book yourselves?
Yes. Every single word. That might be hard to believe considering Rosie often asks me what she should write when she needs to sign her name, but it's true.

What did you set out to achieve?
We wanted to provide comfort to those who needed it. We wanted to make people laugh and feel part of a safe community.

Would you ever write another book?
Yes, I'm looking forward to writing my first fiction piece, *When Harry Met Stally*.

What was the most challenging aspect of writing the book?
Writing the book.

Describe this book in three words.
Girl make thought.

What separates this book from any other YouTuber books?
It's yellow.

Sell me this book!
'This book is brought to you by Best Fiends.'

Where is the weirdest place you wrote this book?
We wrote a lot of it when we were touring North America!
People had no idea we had so many projects on at the
same time and I don't think I've EVER been so stressed! But
taking our live show to Canada and the US was unforgettable, especially as I can remember where I was, the feelings
I felt and the memories I made when I was simultaneously
writing the book!

What was the worst part of writing the book?
Knowing what to include. It was tough for me to discuss
suicidal thoughts but I treated it like my own therapy!
Sharing can be really scary, but now I've achieved an even
greater sense of closure just by opening up about it. You'd
assume it would aggravate old wounds, but for me I was
able to put it all to bed, and now I eagerly await my next
breakdown for the sequel to this book, *Over It*.

How was it writing a book with your other half?
Rosie and I work extremely well together. We always have!
It's a relationship that just works. We have the same goal: to
be proud of the content we create. Whether it's in video
format, live performances, book-writing or awards acceptance speeches (humble brag: minus one point and go back
to the start), we put everything into each project to ensure
our audience is getting the very best of us.

**Be honest. Did you secretly do more work than
Rosie?**
Yes.

What are you going to do with all your free time now you've finished the book?
Train ants to carry me to the fridge.

Do you think you will ever read a book again?
I've only ever finished one book in my life. Not because I don't like to read, but because nothing seems to hold my interest! The only book I HAVE finished is *Twilight: New Moon*. Not because it was particularly well written but because I was intrigued to find out if Jacob was a lesbian.

How do you think you will feel when you see your book in the shops?
Well, I'm hoping I won't see any because they'll have sold out, but so proud and thankful that we were able to have this opportunity in the first place! I can't wait to walk into every retailer, pick up our book and place it at the front of every shelf. And if it's in a section with other YouTuber books, I'll accidentally relocate all the other books into Children's Early Learning.

Coming Out

Now, I'm not assuming that all of you fall under the LGBT umbrella, but I think now's a good time to reiterate a few things. I never had too much of an internal struggle when I realised I was gay. I never had a problem with it, but I feared others might. That was my biggest concern: being rejected by the people I loved. I wanted to invite them into my life so that they could be a part of it. I swear to God, coming out can be one of the hardest things any LGBT person will do. It's a monumental moment which is totally life-changing. Some people spend the majority of their lives plucking up the courage to do it, while for others it's far less traumatic. The point is, it's different for everyone. I wish we didn't live in an age when we can still be made to feel ashamed or guilty for loving another human. It's nonsensical to me how that could ever cause offence. I will never understand how love can be harmful to anyone, or can be hated, measured or dismissed. As far as we know, we only live once, so why on earth would anyone want to spend their one life trying to prevent other people from being happy?

To anyone struggling with being gay, whether it's the shame it can bring, or the fear that you'll lose your friends and family, let me tell you something. Even in the worst-case scenario of your fears being realised, there is another family waiting for you at the end of the rainbow. Just follow the Yellow Brick Road. I truly mean it. Adulthood allows you to form a chosen family, and there's nothing like surrounding yourself with like-minded people who have gone through everything you're going through.

Whatever your background, your beliefs or your upbringing, love is love. Love is a positive and powerful force and when it's shared between two people – any two people – it should be celebrated. Love cannot cause harm to anyone outside of that relationship. What is shameful about love? Nothing. Would you take offence at a mother loving her son? No. Would you take offence at a sister loving her brother? No. Would you take offence at a boy loving a girl? No. So why is love between two people who are the same sex any different? Gender has no bearing on love. Sex between two consenting adults has nothing to do with anyone else, and if it's the physical nature of a same-sex relationship that offends some people, be assured that they're doing all the same stuff in their relationships, so they have no grounds to be bothered.

Growing up, I never even knew a lesbian, let alone had access to the docks where they seem to congregate. Social media barely existed and there was no local or online community I could be a part of. I came from a very white, conservative part of the country, and bless my parents, but they were a little older than those of my peers. There didn't seem to be an option except to stay in the closet until I was confident enough in myself and my surroundings to burst out singing hits from musical theatre.

For some people, internalised homophobia can prevent them from living as their most authentic selves. This breaks my heart. When I was a teenager, and even into my early twenties, clothes shopping was one of my biggest hates. I was never drawn to frills, skirts, dresses, strappy tops, low-cut jeans, or anything that remotely clung to my figure. I had no body confidence, no sense of style, and I couldn't even dream of putting an outfit together. My mum would buy the majority of my clothes because I had a crippling fear that people were judging me for the clothes I was looking at in a shop. I would only ever spend a maximum of ten minutes in each store before I felt uncomfortable and needed to leave. I was completely out of my depth and was worried because I didn't like any of the clothes designed for women. It's only now, as I'm about to embark on my thirties, that I've stopped caring about people's opinions. It took a really long time, and even though I think to some extent we always care a little, it will never stop me from wearing what I want. One thing I've noticed over the last few years is how positively the world has embraced the idea of androgyny and how fashion has moved forward. That's not to say I don't think there's still a place for gender-stereotypical styles – I just think that any gender can wear whatever's available on the spectrum! Men should be able to wear skirts, women should be able to wear suits. We aren't what we wear; we're the way that we treat people. Style is the aesthetic of our personalities, it's our creative expression, but it's not something our souls should be reasured by.

I was always concerned that I'd look 'too lesbian' if I dressed the way I wanted to growing up. I didn't want to give myself away by appearing more masculine than I should have. When I struggled with my OCD before dropping out of sixth-form college, I made sure I picked 'feminine' colours to wear. Pinks, yellows and pastels, to oppress my internal passion for plaid. When I think about how ridiculous this was it frustrates me that I even gave a shit to modify myself for acceptance amongst strangers. Other people were presenting themselves the way they wanted to, so why wasn't I?

The lead-up to coming out can be such an uncomfortable time. Developing your own identity can take decades. Finding out who you are takes courage, determination and resilience. But you have all these things with or without other people's support; you just have to find your strength. And this isn't wishy-washy bullshit, this is real! It's real because I'm not the only one who's said it. I'm not the only one who's told you it gets better. And if you're going through a period in your life when you're not feeling confident, don't be frustrated with yourself. It's a part of the journey. No one experiences life without some insecurities that hold them back. It's a part of your evolution, so allow yourself time to evolve. No one could ever run before they could crawl. It's just not possible to learn without each baby step, and you should never feel embarrassed about your past. Am I embarrassed of my poncho phase? No. Yes. But only because running in one generated an upward force known as 'lift' and with a strong tailwind I started to ascend.

I understand that for some people the reasons not to come out far outweigh the reasons to do so. I could never tell someone that coming out will guarantee happiness if they're living in a country where their lives may be at risk. I can't pretend I know what it's like for absolutely everyone just because I've lived my own story. For those who do decide to stay in the closet, that's entirely their choice and these people should never ever be judged as not being brave or proud enough to come out. Everyone's decision should be respected. But if you are one of these people, know that self-acceptance will take you a long way on the road to happiness. Just because you can't come out, it doesn't mean you can't love yourself, so in spite of your surroundings, never live a life of guilt or shame.

I think it's fair to say that for the majority of people, coming out to their families causes the greatest concern. It's also difficult in the workplace, as most people assume you're straight by default, which can make it tough to know how to correct them. But something I see happening is a greater awareness not to assume before you know. We've advanced in leaps and bounds, not only in the legislation of LGBT marriage around the world, but in advertising, media representation and global support. There are gay churches, gay districts, gay celebrations, and a tonne of gay networks out there to assist anyone who seeks their help. I plan to get involved in a lot more LGBT aid projects in the next few years, because I believe that together we're making a difference!

One question we always get asked is how to come out to friends and family. As you can imagine, without knowing anything about your environment or the people surrounding you, this is a difficult question. Having said that, I've decided to put together a few suggestions of ways to come out that you can pick from to best suit your circumstance. I've put a lot of time into this to make sure I'm guiding you responsibly. So choose carefully, because you can only do this once.

1. Tell them you're gay but not a Fanilow. An excellent method: shocking news swiftly followed by wonderful news. A Barry Manilow fan army is greater cause for alarm than same-sex attraction.

2. Hire Kevin Bacon. Kevin will promote anything. He'll happily deliver the news and will even throw in free data if the reaction wasn't what you'd hoped for.

3. Shave the message into your hair. Ever wondered what the back of your head is for? Free advertising space.

4. Blame them. Tell your parents that being gay is hereditary

and that one of them must be a carrier. As they start to blame each other, steal money from their wallets. If they're not buying it, change your angle and tell them it's down to environmental upbringing. Then ask them where they think they went wrong.

5. Hit them with false statistics. 'Did you know 97 per cent of LGBT teens grow up to be Sir Ian McKellen?'

Dealing with Homophobia

Phobia. An extreme or irrational fear of or aversion to something. Luckily Rosie and I have never had to deal with a serious homophobic attack, but it can happen. Like most prejudices, fear and misunderstanding lead to hatred. You have to remember that not everyone will accept you. That's fine, you can deal with that. You don't accept Jessica Simpson. But like all discrimination, it can be incredibly unpleasant to witness and experience. I'll never forget the reaction I elicited by kissing my girlfriend at Thorpe Park. A group of four boys and a girl were walking behind us and it was the girl who shouted, 'EURGGHHHHHH! Did you see that? That girl kissed another girl! Fucking gross.' I hope they strapped her in correctly when she went on Stealth . . .

I just didn't understand what she found so offensive. Was it *really* that shocking? It wasn't even a prolonged embrace – in fact, I couldn't have kissed her quicker! It's my opinion that she absolutely fucking LOVED IT and didn't know how to react in front of her friends. It's like when you see animals mating at West Midland Safari Park and all you can do is announce it at the top of your lungs! 'OMG! ROSIE, LOOK! THEY'RE DOING IT!' The only reason she added 'Fucking gross' at the end was because she didn't want her male friends to assume she condoned it after pointing it out. Or, it's totally possible it DID gross her out! But like cheese with peanut butter, don't bash it until you've tried it.

I like to think I'm able to turn the other cheek, but I'm not.

Homophobia infuriates me. We used to live by a small convenience store and frequently popped in for milk, eggs, big-brand cereal knock-offs and tasty treats. The shop owner was always pleasant and appreciated our custom, until the day he realised we were living together. I was aggressively interrogated.

'What do you do?'

'We run a business together.'

'You live together?'

'Yes.'

'How long?'

'Two years.'

'Not like *that* though? Because if it was like *that* I'd have to get my gun.'

He wasn't joking. Before now he'd always been eager to touch me at any opportunity he could, which was gross, but now his attitude had changed. What was I supposed to say? 'Yes, we're in love, we're having sex, we run a business from home and we live one door down from you and your gun.' I froze. I couldn't believe that this man was threatening me. I'd never felt so vulnerable. The idea that two women could fall in love without need of a man clearly maddened him, and was something he wished he could stamp out. Needless to say, we never returned to his shop. I still replay the exchange in my head, wishing I'd said or done something different, but at the time I was so shocked by his reaction that I lied and said we were just friends. Am I disappointed with myself? Yes, I am. Would I do the same again? Yes, I would. I'd never encourage anyone to fight the good fight if it puts them in danger, however commendable it may be. Homophobic abuse can really shake you up, and there's nothing shameful in being upset by it! Of course it's going to upset you! You're human! Or possibly the devil, considering you're LGBT, but everyone has feelings!

When I worked at the Apple premium retailer I used to give lessons to a man called Fred. He was great. He was elderly, he had brilliant stories and he was a super-fast learner! We got on really well, until gay people came up in conversation.

'You have gay friends do you?'

'Yes, I do!'

'And you're all right with that are you?'

'Yeah, I love them, they're great!'

Instead of telling Fred I myself was gay, I thought it would be best to give him the name of our YouTube channels, considering he had such a vested interest in social media. Before he left that day, I told him to check out our most popular videos. After a year of teaching, I never saw Fred again. After his rant about his disgust for homosexuals, it wouldn't have been easy to rely on one to help him understand iTunes. It's a shame, I would have been totally up for having a discussion with him. I was forgiving because he'd clearly adopted an unwarranted disdain for gay people because he'd never met one before (or assumed he hadn't), and fear leads to hate, hate leads to aggression, and aggression led to Fred never learning how to create a playlist. So who suffered the most here? It was Fred.

Fortunately none of these experiences have ever made me doubt myself. Anyone who believes gay people are perverse or evil are just fucking ridiculous. There are perverse and evil heterosexual people, so what makes *them* the way they are? It makes no rational or conceivable sense. This was something that used to provoke my OCD tremendously. But love can never be evil, and that's the bottom line. I'm sure throughout your life you'll have to deal with ignorance like this, but don't let it stop you celebrating yourself: you have every right to live your truth. In the end it'll only make you stronger.

ROSIE
Biphobia

Ah, finally! It's my time to shine. Biphobia. If you are reading this you are either bisexual and could do with a morale boost (couldn't we all?) *or* you are not bi, in which case, at some point in your life you may have been unintentionally biphobic. That's OK. We've all been ignorant and we aren't our past but we are our present. So let's get down to the nitty gritty, shall we?

I have been physically pushed around, slut-shamed, name-called, dismissed, put down and stereotyped, all because I happened to be born with the capacity to love two or more genders. For me personally, I'm into men and women. That's a part of me that is unchangeable, and why on earth would I want to change myself even if I could? So let's get a few things straight (LOL).

Yes, I'm still bisexual even though I'm married to a woman and in a same-sex relationship. The relationship doesn't change the fact that I'm bisexual. Stop arguing with me and get over it. The same goes for people who are bisexual but haven't acted upon it, and for people who are bisexual in a straight relationship. If someone says they are bisexual, immediately jumping on them and questioning their own label isn't the most educated thing to do.

No, bisexuals aren't greedy, and we don't need to make a choice. What we need is for people to stop commenting on how we need to 'pick a side' so we can get on with living our lives.

Bisexuals aren't half straight and half gay, though you sometimes make us feel that way by not accepting us fully into the straight community and not deeming us 'gay enough' to be fully accepted into the gay community either! We are the Hufflepuffs of the LGBT world, cast aside when we just want an equal shot at the Quidditch cup. Is that too much to ask?

So what if you're a bisexual who isn't yet out to friends and family? Or perhaps you're questioning whether you're truly bisexual. There are so many labels now, you may wonder if you're gay, pansexual, or just bi-curious. You may not want to give yourself a label at all, and that's fine too! No one is forcing you to label yourself.

Let's take this step by step.

Am I bisexual?

No one can answer this question but you. Not the answer you were looking for, I'm sure, but it's true. But I can give you some tips to send you in the right direction. If you think you have a romantic interest in two or more genders you could be bisexual. I've had a lot of people say to me, 'I like guys *and* girls but I've only been with girls and I like them a LOT more. Does that make me bisexual?' You don't have to like two or more genders equally to be bisexual. It doesn't have to be a totally equal split. A bisexual could like guys a little and girls a LOT or vice versa and still be bi. I know it can seem confusing, but listen, there's no pressure to understand everything right away! There are people who don't even realise they aren't straight until they're retired! We live in such a heteronormative world, it's OK if you are 'late' figuring stuff out, or are simply taking your time.

Let's take a deep breath and go through the facts. It doesn't matter who you are attracted to or who you fall for. You can take as long as you like to get to a place where you feel confident with who you are. And if you decide to ditch the labels and go with the flow? That's OK too. I find that you can over-analyse anything if you're too focused on it. So take a step back and make sure you aren't getting so caught up in your own sexuality that you're forgetting to enjoy life. Sexuality is just ONE of the many aspects that make you who you are. Yes, it's important, but it isn't your only defining feature. You are a beautiful, multi-faceted human being. Everyone deserves to feel confident, loved and happy. So I would give your feelings some thought, but try not to ruminate. Be like Pocahontas, go wherever the wind takes you. Remember, you're in control here. You get to decide how you feel, if you want to share those feelings with anyone and when you would like to do so.

I think I've figured it out . . . but how can I accept myself?

Good question! First of all, a great place to start is to stop assuming that everybody else in life has everything together and is totally confident and accepting of themselves. You are not alone in this. In fact, I'd say that most people have to go through many phases of self-acceptance throughout their lifetime. As people, we are constantly evolving. I am continually accepting the new things I learn about myself. I think it's common knowledge that if you have love and acceptance for yourself, it will make everything else in life a little easier. But how do we do it? I would suggest we start by not being so self-critical. We can be our own worst critics. Treat yourself how you would treat others going through a hard time. Give yourself plenty of compassion, patience and kindness. It's the perfect way to start.

I'm scared of coming out

That's OK and is totally understandable. Most people have felt the same way. I can't tell you whether or not it is right for you to come out at this point; that's up to you. You need to feel ready. And it's also OK not to feel ready. I know a huge part of Rose's coming out story was that she accepted she was gay, but didn't tell people right away. She was just content understanding that that was who she was. Then later she decided to tell people who were close friends, who she felt had earned the privilege.

Unfortunately, I can't predict how the people you come out to will react. I also know that although close family and friends are the people we focus on coming out to, further down the line you will continue to come out. I've had to tell doctors and nurses. Introduce Rose to friends of family. It's OK, you get used to it. But let's get back to the basics.

Telling your friends and family

I always tell people that if your friends don't like you because of your sexuality then they're not really your friends. But what if you get a negative reaction from your family? Trust me, I completely understand the feeling of family rejection. During the writing of this book, my stepfather of twenty years cut off all contact with me. (You know you're living life right when you lose not one but TWO father figures! No, but seriously . . .) The fear of your family, the people you love and cherish, rejecting you is awful. So let's take a look at some examples to put your mind at ease.

CASE STUDY I: ROSE'S MUM

It took Rose's a mum a little time to come to terms with having a gay daughter and also to accept me into the family. Despite her reservations, she never stopped loving Rose. And despite a rocky beginning, she now proudly tells everyone that Rose is gay and that I am her daughter-in-law. It's all about how we choose to communicate. We should always try to understand where the other person is coming from. It'll often be the case that any negativity actually comes from concern. What this case study shows is that even in the event of an initial negative response, things always have a chance of getting better with time, patience and understanding. Remember, you've had time to come to terms with your sexuality, while your parents and family members have not. Just as you needed to think things through and accept yourself, so might they. There are things they might be worried about, like whether you'll be discriminated against now that you're out, or whether it will affect your chances of getting a job. Rose's mum was worried about how Rose being gay would affect her chances in life, and that concern came from a place of love.

CASE STUDY 2: MY MUM

My mum, without meaning to, totally erased my bisexuality and made me feel pretty stupid, naive and small. Luckily, I'm a strong person who had inner self-confidence to see me through, but I realise that not everybody can be so self-assured, and one knock-back could seriously damage your confidence. I told my mum I was bisexual at the ripe old age of fifteen and I can remember exactly what happened. She was in the kitchen busy making food, and she refused to make eye contact and totally dismissed it. I felt extremely embarrassed and cringed when I said the word 'bisexual'. The whole thing was painfully awkward, I wish I had the opportunity to relive it differently. Years and years passed and I continued knowing I was bisexual and experimented with girls and boys. As I sat in Malvern spa with my mum I decided to tell her that I had a date with a girl called Rose who was a lesbian. Mum didn't bat an eyelid. Maybe she trusted what I said now that I was older, even though nothing had changed and I was still bisexual. Maybe she had evolved and learned more about bisexuality. Or maybe, because she was chilling in a relaxed environment, she had more head space to digest it and react better. Who knows? Whatever happened, it was positive and she accepted Rose with open arms. She's never said anything ignorant or ill-informed, nor has she questioned my sexuality since. For many people, it just takes a little time to get on board. Allow them that, because it doesn't mean they love you any less.

CASE STUDY 3: MY GRANDAD

My mum had told me not to tell my grandad I was bisexual, and I think it was simply because it was the early days of dating Rose, and my mum had no idea we would end up getting married. I could have ended up with a man, so she saw no point in telling him. It did make me concerned about his reaction though. When my relationship with Rose began to get serious, I started bringing her to family occasions. Someone eventually told him, and he surprised me by being totally cool with it. He always asks after Rose, he came to our wedding, he shook Rose's dad's hand, and he even helped feed our cat while we were getting ready for the big day!

Don't underestimate people. Don't judge them if you don't wish to be judged. Even people from a different generation who are possibly predisposed to a different mindset can get on board!

CASE STUDY 4: BEING OUTED

I hate having to talk about this because I see it as one of the worst offences. Being outed is probably one of the most traumatic things anyone can experience. Not only do we have something so personal to share, but having someone do it without our approval can be unbelievably damaging. It's so important to come out when you're ready. It's a decision that should only ever be made by you. But when we have a secret so important to us which we hold dear, unfortunately it can be seen as ammunition by others.

Some people may consider it merely hot gossip, but either way, it's not their secret to tell. I experienced being outed by my brother, who I don't believe did it to intentionally cause harm. He did it because he didn't realise that my sexuality is my right to share with the people I decide to tell. He went to a family gathering on my dad's side, and I came up in conversation. Aunties and uncles were naturally asking after me and my brother told them that I was in a relationship with Rose. I was NOT happy. In fact, writing about it is making me angry again, LOL.

My father doesn't have a relationship with me, so I didn't feel it was his business to know who I was having relationships with. I didn't want him knowing my sexuality because I don't feel he has a right to judge me. He is not involved in my life. I don't care for his approval or disapproval. I was really angry that a bunch of people I barely knew had been told this information without my consent. But my brother didn't mean to betray confidences. In fact, he was probably proud of me and felt like there wasn't anything to hide.

Some people get outed in much worse ways: rumours spread around school, being outed to your immediate family. It's a frustrating and unfair situation. All I can suggest you do is tell only those you trust the most, and explain that it is your right to decide how many and which people you would like to tell.

'Why is society still so annoying about it?'

I know, right? Come on, society, haven't you read Chapter 6 yet?

Although society has a long way to go, I've seen major improvements. More people are getting clued up about this stuff. More and more people are coming out. All you can do is love yourself, and trust your gut. The positive side of this situation is that you might have a wonderful coming-out process. Your friends and family might be completely understanding and supportive. Yes, there's a possibility that it won't go quite as smoothly as you'd hope, but all we can do is gently educate and inform, and continue to be true to ourselves. Ditch friends who contribute to any negativity, unless you can educate them to think otherwise. Remember, you are a wonderful, unique person and you deserve the same treatment as everyone else.

'But the thing is, you say all this stuff about bisexuals but the ONE time I dated a bisexual they cheated on me and broke my heart!'

That person didn't break your heart because they were bisexual; they broke your heart because they're a heart-breaker! If you really think bisexuals are responsible for all the heartbreak in the world, tell me, how come your other relationships didn't work out? Is your mum bisexual? Is that the reason your parents got divorced? Come on. Even I can figure this stuff out and I think the moon is a conspiracy theory.

'OK, maybe you've got a point . . . So what now?'

Try to be less judgemental. Let people identify as whatever sexuality or gender they're comfortable with! Don't question everyone else's reasoning for what they do in their own life. Take a CHILL PILL. (If you don't understand that reference it's because I'm old and that's what we used to say in the nineties.)

'OK, cool. Can you name some famous bisexuals that I can look up to and adore?'

Evan Rachel Wood, Lady Gaga, Lauren Jauregui, Michelle Rodriguez, Cynthia Nixon . . . amongst countless others!

'Wait, one more thing . . . Does your wife not get really sick of you talking about men all the time?'

Rose gets jealous when I talk about guys but that's our kink. But I'm mildly outraged at your assumption that men are a huge talking point for me.

> **'Wow, OK, then. So I guess everything's working out nicely for you.'**
> Yeah, it's going pretty well. I'm confrontationally educating people, and everyone knows the most effective way to teach is through aggression.

ROSE

Guys, I was thinking about how we could end this book and I came up with two viable options. One: to include a picture of me adjacent to a picture of Rosie, asking you to circle our weakest physical attributes. Then I was told that although that's fun for the reader, it conflicts with the messaging in Chapter 6. So I've decided to incorporate a multiple-choice test instead! Now don't panic. There's actually no way you can fail this test – it's more of a personality quiz based on the things you've learned! We're going to start off easy and gravitate towards slightly trickier scenarios. Don't look at anybody else's answers because you're only cheating yourself.

I hope you've enjoyed *Overshare* as much as I've enjoyed writing 80 per cent of it. Just kidding, Rosie's written half. Not that an unequal input would mean she's any less a contributor. You can still be called an author with a contribution of 1 per cent or 100 per cent. Writing is a spectrum, and it's a common misconception that co-writing is 50/50. Rosie should never be branded greedy if she were to write more. She was just born with the capacity to be both motivated and lazy, and she doesn't have to pick a side.

R&R Personality Quiz

1. Your best friend confides in you and tells you she's bisexual. How do you react?

A. Tell her she just doubled her options

B. Assume it's a come-on

C. Tell her it's now more likely she'll sleep with someone she's unknowingly related to

2. You've just come out to your parents. They reacted badly. What do you do?

A. Grow in your eyebrows until they join in the middle

B. Replace the sugar with salt

C. Download gay pornography onto your father's laptop and start pointing fingers

3. Your friends drop you and you're unsure of the reason. Do you . . .

A. Subtweet about loyalty

B. Have an honest conversation

C. Who cares?

4. You're trying to make it on YouTube but your channel isn't growing. Do you . . .

A. Upload Superkiss

B. Date Stevie Boebi

C. Attend YouTube conventions and pretend to care about your audience

5. A man talks down to you, assuming you won't understand. Do you . . .

A. Play dead

B. Agree that women have problems understanding their native language

C. Put him on your Instastory and make it go viral

6. You think you might be suffering from obsessive compulsive disorder. Do you . . .

A. Remain thankful you're not Carly Rae Jepson

B. Make it your brand

C. Obsess about it and prove yourself right

7. You're not sure whether or not to have children. You should only become a parent if . . .

A. You have a husband to rely on

B. You're willing to love them unconditionally

C. You're able to sell them

8. You've developed romantic feelings for your straight best friend. Do you . . .

A. Take it to your grave

B. Take a leap of faith

C. Get a job to pay for your therapy

9. You've been outed by a friend. What do you do next?

A. Hide in Mexico

B. Comfort eat

C. Listen to Demi Lovato

10. You're about to meet your idol. Do you . . .
A. Make sure Liam Payne fucks off
B. Avoid all eye contact
C. Try to slip them your number

Now tally up your answers!

IF YOU'VE TICKED MOSTLY As:
You're what us professionals call a Type A personality. Friends are important to you, which is why you make out with them. They're receptive but you both know your limits. You're keen to explore your sexuality and even though you're not into labels, you identify as supersexual, also known as bi, pan or poly, though you're not one to use a label that already exists. You appreciate that women aren't possessions yet you own a few. Entrepreneurial! You carefully consider how you present yourself and your keen eye for fashion has put you on the radar for YouTube sponsorship deals. Now you're earning that coin by promoting a skin brush that doesn't work, your foot is solidly through the door! In spite of your promiscuity, you're one to hold back when it comes to intimacy. And although you disdain her, sometimes you wish you had the fringe of Carly Rae Jepson to hide your feelings behind.

IF YOU'VE TICKED MOSTLY Bs:
You're a little dense. That's OK, we live in a world where we're taught to accept people's flaws no matter what. You're a believer in true love, but only if it's financially beneficial. You're strongly attracted to people who can open doors for you and friends describe you as a risk-taker. You're opportunistic, and some may cast you in a negative light for it, but

you're laughing all the way to the bank! You're not overly liked by most, but the friends you do have are loyal and true. You regard them as Hufflepuffs and decide to abuse their good nature, and rightly so. You have few morals, but why be weighed down by a conscience when you could be making money? One thing's for sure, you're going to make an excellent parent. By selling out you've provided a college fund for your future children and the prospect of a bright future. You're going to be a fantastic momager.

IF YOU'VE TICKED MOSTLY Cs:
You just don't give a fuck do you? I like you. You're confident, smart, seductive, hot-tempered, difficult to tame, problematic, flirtatious, but deep down you're surprisingly pure. You're Rosie. Don't be alarmed, this isn't necessarily a hindrance. You may scream at nothing, but your prospects in life are huge! You see something you want and you get it. No matter the obstacles! Whether it's maths or homelessness, your determination and inner strength always take you to where you need to be. You're tenacious, and people may fear that, especially your parents who consider you their biggest regret. But you find solace in the Lovatic fandom and you support Demi even more than her bra.

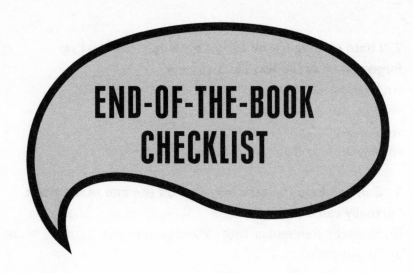

END-OF-THE-BOOK CHECKLIST

ROSIE

Dear reader. It is with a heavy heart that I must now inform you that we have in fact reached the end. I understand how you must be feeling – that bittersweet sensation of enlightenment at what you've read and grief over the fact that there is no more. There may even be a tiny Rose and Rosie book-shaped hole left in your heart, that nothing other than a second Rose and Rosie book could ever fill. But panic not. We care about our audience and have prepared for this exact moment. Below is a checklist that will help you survive the end of the book.

You can go through the checklist step by step to whip you back into shape and to get you ready for our next video!

I. Are you already experiencing Rose and Rosie comedown?

YES ☐ Read the book again or head over to our YouTube channel.

NO ☐ You must have misunderstood the question.

2. 'I hate coming to the end of the book. It's like I've forgotten what life was like before it!'

Understandable. Here are a few links that might help:

www.youtube.com/RoseEllenDix

www.youtube.com/TheRoxetera

www.youtube.com/LetsPlayGamesWithoutSkills

3. 'Can you help me take my mind off the end of the book, I actually can't cope.'

No problem. Remember that time Shannon and Cammie broke up? It was awful.

4. Can't you just keep writing?

No, we've been doing that since Chapter 2 because we were told we needed more than one chapter.

5. 'I'm beginning to feel much better now.'

Good. Now, to round things off, and for you to be able to gently close this book for good, why don't we end on a guessing game? How many secrets did Rose and Rosie actually share in their aptly named book *Overshare*? Have a guess! That's incorrect, but if you'd like to hear more, the best thing to do is leave a five-star rating online, which gives us more leverage for a second book deal.

Right, guys, that's it from us! Don't forget to like, comment and subscribe, and remember, always judge a book by its cover. Bye!